Buster

Buster

The Military Dog Who Saved a Thousand Lives

RAF Police Flight Sergeant
Will Barrow

As Told to Isabel George

Thomas Dunne Books
St. Martin's Press
New York

THOMAS DUNNE BOOKS.
An imprint of St. Martin's Press.

The views and opinions expressed in this book are those of the author alone and should not be taken to represent those of HMG, MOD, the RAF, or any government agency.

RAF Police Flight Sergeant Will Barrow is named on the front cover of this book. This is the account of his and Buster's story, as told to Isabel George. RAF Police Flight Sergeant Will Barrow has not received any personal financial reward through his involvement with this book.

www.thomasdunnebooks.com
www.stmartins.com

The Library of Congress Cataloging-in-Publication Data is available upon request

ISBN 978-1-250-07646-5 (hardcover)
ISBN 978-1-4668-8786-2 (e-book)

First published in Great Britain by Virgin Books, an imprint of Ebury Publishing, a division of Penguin Random House

First U.S. Edition: October 2015

10 9 8 7 6 5 4 3 2 1

To Izzy for her hard work, Tracy and my family for their unwavering support and all military working dog handlers and their fantastic dogs, especially those who have made the ultimate sacrifice for Queen and country.

Contents

Prologue

'Buster, where the bloody hell are you?'

I had no idea why I said that. I knew that Buster would be no more than a whisker's width away from me. I heard him sigh as if to say, 'For goodness' sake, mate, just calm down. We're out for a ride that's all.' But that's Buster's view on the world. Even in this inky blackness, as we sat in the belly of a Viking armoured vehicle, he would be thinking he was just out on a trip with his friends and, if he was lucky, one or two of them might have a bit of food to share. After all, this dog was already a veteran of two tours of Bosnia. If the journey ended with a long walk, then this boring sitting-still bit would have all been worth it.

It was early in our relationship, and I realised how jealous I was becoming of Buster's simple logic. That morning we were up at 0300. An hour and fifteen minutes later we were kitted and booted, and rooted to the spot by the sound of something very solid heading our way. The earth shook under our feet, and while Buster sat in a Sunday morning kind of pose, wondering if the early start meant a second breakfast, I studied the dark horizon for clues. Suddenly, the entire perimeter of Forward Operating Base (FOB) Price was blindingly illuminated, and for a few seconds Buster and I stood like a pair of startled rabbits. We were witnessing the arrival of the Viking troop of the Royal Marines.

The convoy had driven for two hours overnight from Camp Bastion. Relying entirely on their night vision goggles to cover the distance, the drivers brought the vehicles through the darkness to the base's main gates before switching to full beam. Winding down to the harbour, the Vikings came to an ear-splitting halt with the screech of their metal tracks.

Vikings are huge, ugly, tracked armoured vehicles. They come in two parts. The front has a can for the driver, commander and gunner. The gunner is stood with his head out of a hatch in the top and armed with a general purpose machine gun (GPMG or 'Gimpy') or a .50 calibre heavy machine gun (HMG), both of which will ruin your day. Behind this is a powerful engine that propels it along at speed. The rear compartment is for troops or supplies. It will seat six people, but any more than four is pretty uncomfortable. As usual, everything is covered in sand and dust, which has to be constantly cleaned out.

At this time, the Vikings were feared by the Taliban, and this morning's had come to collect me and Buster and deliver us to our unit in the field. True to form, Buster sprang into action, meeting and greeting the guys who clearly looked a lot less boring than me. Panting and wagging his stumpy tail, he leapt into the Viking ready for another mini-adventure packed with fresh smells, noises and voices.

Despite the gloominess inside, I knew Buster could see me, but his focus would be on getting a seat. As the engine rumbled away I quickly dealt with the practical side of things such as storing our bags. My bulging Bergan was full of Buster's food, but the marine sergeant lifted it onto his shoulder as if it was a child's lunch box. Tearing open the rear armour-plated door he dropped my stuff into the main compartment.

I crouched down before stepping in to join the heaving, breathing bodies of two hefty Royal Marines in full body armour. I was given a headset so I could hear all communications between the commander, driver and gunner above the noise of the engine in the front can. Buster was already in there somewhere but I couldn't see him on any of the seats. After a little jostling with bags, rifles and body mass, I sat and shuffled my feet to create some personal space and some Buster space. No one knew how long the journey to the patrol area was going to take. Christ it was getting hot and I knew Buster must be feeling the heat too. 'It's OK pal ... don't worry,' I said, hoping my voice was steady. But I think I needed the reassurance more than he did.

After a short while we joined Highway 1, a decent 'proper' road by local standards, which encircles Afghanistan. Suddenly I realised that this was it. I couldn't escape now, even if I wanted to. And I admit that there were times as I packed, unpacked and re-packed my kit for the umpteenth time that I had thought of taking an immediate career break.

OK, where are you Buster? I pushed my right foot in front of me: it connected with something soft but solid – Buster. Buster didn't like sitting on the floor. In fact Buster never sat on the floor. He preferred to commandeer a seat next to the guys – not necessarily next to me I might add.

I bent down and whispered in his ear, 'Just checking in case you have found the only clever dick in this sweaty space that has a ham bone or a chew stick about his person. I know what you're like,' I ruffled his ears, 'you think I'm just a thick human being, but I know what you're thinking and what's more I thank God for you, you great daft dog.'

Those who aren't dog lovers probably think that talking to our four-legged friends is a step too close to crazy, but sometimes there's no better conversationalist than a dog: if you are afraid they sense it and calm you without uttering a word. If you are making a fool of yourself they draw you to one side and give you that look that says 'you know, you can be a real prat sometimes'. And if you are lost for words they fill the silence by giving you a big kiss. As Buster leant his warm spaniel body into my leg I felt a swell of reassurance wash over me. I knew that if I died tonight I would not be alone because my best pal would be watching over me.

We drove for some time, the light slowly coming up. I was at the back and had a small window to look through. Most of the time there was nothing of interest to see, but occasionally we would pass through a small town.

Ping! Ping! Ping!

A hail of metal-on-metal shots splattered against the Viking.

Spat, spat, spat!

I stayed low and arched over Buster, who was panting like crazy. I put my hand to his chest and I could feel his heart pounding. For what was probably only seconds I left my hand where it was, so I would know if he was hit. While I knew in my head that there was no need to worry, as there was no way that normal bullets would penetrate the beast that was the Viking, my heart still made me pull him close to me to protect him.

'Is everyone OK?' The driver's voice came through the headset loud and clear. I opened my mouth to answer but that's as far as I got before another voice interrupted.

'You cheeky bastards. Have this you shitheads. You won't like it but you're getting it!' The vehicle shook as the gunner let off a burst of rapid fire from his Gimpy.

We were blind to the action, holed up the Viking's belly, and captive to whatever happened next. 'Drive on, damn it!' The commander's voice boomed down the headset to the driver, but the gunner, in the most vulnerable position with his head and shoulders well above the single turret, was determined to give as good as the vehicle got.

'Fuck off boss, we can't let 'em get away with that. Have a bit more. Go on ... take that you bastards!'

One more burst of retaliation from the machine gun ended the insurgents' attack as suddenly as it had started. We stayed deep down in the Viking's belly, no longer just a confined sweat pit but now a cocoon-like protective metal box. Buster was looking very relaxed and matter-of-fact about being under fire, but I still leant over and ran my hands over his silky coat and ruffled his floppy ears before sitting back and reflecting on the last few minutes of my life. As we wrestled to re-arrange our weapons and belongings that had been thrown about in the fray, Buster saw his window of opportunity to take the vacant seat in front of the narrow slit window at the rear. From there he calmly watched our attackers disappear into the glow of dawn.

For Buster and me it was our first experience of a Taliban ambush. We'd arrived in the country just a few days before, and I knew it was only a taste of worse to come. I took a deep breath. I'm sure Buster did too, in his canine way. I was glad that it was over but I got the distinct impression that the marines in the back felt cheated about not getting into a scrap. There were mutterings of, 'Wouldn't have minded the chance to kick the shit out of them,' and, 'Just, get back here you bastards,' and the like.

The frustration of having to sit and hear the action and not be able to get involved was hurting them, I could tell. They were all honed combat veterans coming to the end of their tour. All lean, slightly fidgety and their sand-blasted fatigues were customised in the way we do on tour, with nicknames finding their way onto badges and insignia and permanent-markered onto helmets, 'The Taliban Hunting Club' being among the favourites. They were not just unafraid of confrontation, they were constantly up for it, and disappointed when they couldn't get at it.

Buster shifted his bottom from side to side to sweep up more of the space he had made for himself between two of the men. It was like watching an embarrassing relative shove people out of the way on a bus, but I didn't want to stop him, especially as everyone else thought it was funny. Clearly, if something else kicked off Buster didn't want to be the one on the floor covered in bags and boots as everything shifted around. I reached into my Bergan for a bottle of water and as I turned to face him, bottle at the ready, I glimpsed one of the burly soldiers stretching his fingers towards Buster. I sat still, not wanting to disturb the moment, especially as the soft old dog saw what was needed and obliged by stretching forward to offer his slobbering muzzle.

'Is the dog OK? That's the main thing,' boomed the sergeant, who dragged a massive sun-burnished arm over his brow to divert a river of perspiration. He was in his mid-twenties and massively built; I was glad he was one of us. 'Good job he doesn't mind a bit of noise this one. Right attitude for the job. I've got a springer at home but I'm not sure he would have acted like an OAP on a sightseeing trip like this one. Good lad.'

Buster was still enjoying the attention of the marine who had gone from reaching out to tickle Buster's ears to a full belly rub. Turns out he once had a dog just like Buster.

'All good with the dog,' I said.

CHAPTER 1

A Great Dog

Just five months before we found ourselves in the belly of a Viking under fire, I was on a specialist police dog course at the Defence Animal Centre in Melton Mowbray in spring 2007 when I was approached about a new assignment. They wanted to utilise the exceptional tracking capability of the RAF police dogs in Afghanistan, and the provost marshal's dog Inspector wanted me to head the team. This particular idea was soon canned as tracking in that environment was going to prove too problematic and dangerous. However, I was still going out – but as an Arms and Explosives Search (AES) dog handler instead. This was more within my area of expertise.

When I joined the RAF Police at eighteen I knew that I was destined to be a military working dog handler, and I was right. After an 'apprenticeship' of twelve years with German shepherd patrol dogs, more affectionately known in the trade as 'flesh seeking missiles' and 'furry crocodiles' I moved on through the ranks with drug and detection dogs and then on to arms and explosives search dogs. The job was taking me all over the world but not always to the safest places. I had served in Northern Ireland on two separate tours and done a tour of Bosnia. They had both had their moments of excitement and dread, but I knew this was going to be totally different. I didn't quite know how different though. I had heard stories from my wife Tracy who is also in the RAF and other colleagues about Iraq, but this was going to be like nothing else ever.

All I needed was the right dog. Course over in late June, I returned to RAF Waddington (that's 'Waddo' to anyone in the service) in Lincolnshire, the headquarters of No5 RAF Police Squadron, where I was Senior NCO in charge of the Dog Section and Squadron Dog Inspector, and started asking around.

There's a certain type of dog required for Afghanistan. The desert terrain, the heat and the fact it was a war zone would require a dog with loads of drive and an exceptional nose. The dog would need not just to cope but thrive. There were several arms and explosive search dogs in the RAF system at the time, but I needed a dog that had the vital combination of battle experience and high drive. When you are out with soldiers on patrol, and it's your dog's job to go up front, you need that dog to be focused and driven. A search dog without drive is about as useful as a car without an engine.

If you're anywhere near a group of military dog handlers you will overhear plenty of dog talk. The good dogs, the bad dogs and even the indifferent dogs make their mark on a handler. If you share everything from your food and your friends to your bed, in the shadow of war, bonding is inevitable. But it's the dogs with personality – the ones who are almost human and challenge you as you journey together – that really carve an imprint on your soul. They are the ones you grow and learn with, and the ones who get to know you more than you know yourself. They are the ones you trust with your life when mortality stares you in the face.

It was early July and I called Corporal Nick Lyons, one of my handler pals, whose recommendations were always spot on. He immediately suggested his dog.

'Buster is three years old and has two tours of Bosnia-Herzegovina to his name. He's a bloody good dog and his work rate is second to none. Will, if you're looking for a great dog for a demanding job this is the one you want.'

It may seem strange to some that Nick would so willingly offer up such a special dog, especially one who was clearly so close to his heart. But the fact was that Buster was a working dog, not Nick's pet. Nick knew all too well that Buster had to go where he was needed, for the greater good. And as a career dog, it's what Buster would have wanted too. That didn't mean it was going to be easy to say goodbye.

Nick and Buster were stationed at *HMS Caledonia*, now *MOD Caledonia*, the Royal Navy base in Rosyth, where the dog was assigned to the RAF Special Investigations Branch. I had to see this dog – he sounded like the only one for the job – so the next day I headed up to Scotland with the hope of bringing him home with me.

I told a few colleagues that I was going to meet Buster and I suddenly found myself inundated with testimonials. He was quick, efficient, dedicated and a bloody excellent worker, but when I heard, 'Buster? Oh he is a great dog and a true pal,' I knew he was a bit special. After a six-hour drive, my expectations were high.

Nick had suggested we meet a short distance from the base, where there was an area for Buster to run around and play. I could see him in action and get to know him a little – well as much as you can in an hour or so. I saw that Nick's dog van was already parked up and waiting, so I pulled up alongside it and had a quick look through the window, but Buster must have been in the back.

I already felt a bit sorry for Nick. He had served with Buster in Bosnia, and was about to give up what sounded like the dog of his career. All handlers think their dog is the best but I could tell that Nick was not just proud of this dog, clearly in awe of the dog's skills in the field, but he liked him too, like a mate.

Buster, by all accounts, was a 'character' and in the job we are very aware of the interpretation of 'character'. In my experience that can mean anything from a loveable creature that licks your face and brings you your slippers at the end of a hard day, to a hard-arse heap of solid muscle that would eat your face and your slippers all at the same time. I was guessing that, at best, Buster fell somewhere between the two.

Nick went to the back of the van and out jumped Buster. When I saw him jogging towards me I couldn't help smiling.

'So you're the famous Buster?' I said out loud, as I met the soft brown eyes of the handsome chunk of springer spaniel in front of me. 'Now, are you going to lick me or bite me fella, because I've been told you can do both pretty well?'

He didn't know me well enough to nip me so he just collected a helping of fuss from me instead.

He sat in front of me looking every inch a dog you would choose for a special operation. To be honest, I had never really thought about a dog having military bearing until I set eyes on Buster. Head held high, chest thrust forward, body weight resting back on his hind quarters, he was definitely sitting to attention. He looked proud and wise, and I was beginning to see why the men who knew this dog had so much respect for him. Then he lifted his liver-coloured head and, like a brigadier casting his eye over a raw recruit, he threw me a look and shook his head.

'Oh don't worry, he does that!' said Nick. 'It's his little joke. He's a good all-rounder this one, Will. He's not just good at his job but he's a good lad, if you know what I mean? But you have to be one step ahead of him as he's been here before and knows all the ropes and all the tricks, as I'm sure you will find out.'

The military lists its working dogs as 'equipment', but for a handler out in theatre, in a war zone, their dog is much more than a machine with a heart. A dog is a companion by day and by night. I wanted to get to know Buster, so after all the usual dog handler banter Nick suggested we run him and his other dog, Sprout.

Like a wild thing released, Buster dashed off the lead and tore into the grass with his chocolate nose sniffing over the sweet earth and his powerful hind legs kicking up the turf. He had all the moves of a dog who felt he owned the place, and I felt guilty that in about an hour's time I would be taking him away from Nick and all that was familiar to him.

To give Buster a good workout in one of his favourite places, Nick suggested we gather up the dogs for the ride to the coast. I saw Buster sitting in the front of the van looking out of the window and taking in the scenery. He must have recognised the route and as we got closer to the water he did just as Nick predicted; he started a frantic little dance and his lips wobbled as he let out a little whining noise like a crazy spaniel speak.

Seeing Buster swim that day is something I will never forget. Unless I'm very much mistaken, I'm sure he smiled as he threw himself into the ripples. Catching the salt in his nostrils he started a pattern of dipping in and out of the chilly, grey water and then checking back every now and again with Nick just to make sure it was OK to go back for more.

It was a lovely summer afternoon, warm and still.

Perfect for a visit to the coast and watching the dogs just enjoy being dogs in the sparkling depths. When Nick gave me the nod that it was time to go, I walked towards Buster who was totally immersed, except for his silky auburn head, which frequently bobbed to the surface. The swim was a good idea – a sure way of guaranteeing Buster would be exhausted for the journey to his new home. Better for him if he could sleep most of the way.

Nick called to Buster who turned a deaf ear a couple of times before he eventually dragged himself onto dry land and shook his dripping coat, right to the tip of his stumpy tail. He sat at Nick's feet while his lead was re-attached.

'Well, here he is,' Nick handed me the lead. 'And I'm sorry to say,' he added, 'he's all yours. Look after him for me, won't you? Because I know he will look after you.'

As Nick walked away I looked down to the end of the lead at the brown-flecked chunky dog. He was sitting proud, his forelegs positioned neatly together and his feet turned outwards like a bow-legged ballet dancer.

'Look at you, you bandy-legged sod,' I said, hoping he didn't understand me. 'Hey, never mind mate, the rest of you looks alright. Come on, let's get going. We've got a long journey ahead.'

Buster shifted around to keep an eye on Nick and Sprout, who were now standing together. I guessed they would stay there until we were out of sight. Caught up in the emotional goodbye, I let Buster sit in the van with me. He was wearing an expression that I would see on several occasions in the future, and each time no less heart-wrenching.

As I drove away I couldn't help thinking how difficult the handover must have been for Nick. I could see that he was a bit choked and I know how that feels. I've had to say goodbye to several working dogs in my career, and it's easier with some than others. Most times the split comes after a tour of duty, when the dog enters quarantine and the handler goes on leave. When you find a dog that is special, being forced to let go, with the whole thing being out of your control, is just dreadful. There's only one thing worse, and that's the heartbreak of seeing that special dog working with someone else. It's like seeing your wife with another bloke!

That said, emotional outbursts aren't welcome in the mess. Let's just say it takes a dog handler to know a dog handler. I empathised with Nick completely that day.

After several stops along the way we reached Scotch Corner, our final comfort break. I wandered off with Buster, who was happy for the chance to stretch his legs. He jogged along, gazing at the ground, and I guessed he wasn't ready to have a conversation with me yet. I decided to let him do his own thing and not make a fuss. He would come round in his own time. And besides there was another priority – I needed something to eat.

I was tired and the service station didn't offer a

vast choice of meals so I settled for a quick and tasty burger, which, after an afternoon by the sea, smelled absolutely delicious. As I took my first bite I had an idea. I know it's not a dog treat that anyone, especially a vet, would recommend, but I needed to offer Buster the hand of friendship – what better way than to offer it holding a burger?

I went back to the van where Buster was pretending to be fast asleep. His nose twitched and in an instant his head was off his paws. Eyes wide and not knowing if he needed to sit or stand to get a fix on the source of the warm, meaty smell, Buster jigged about, his ears swishing from side to side.

'So Buster, how's about a quick treat? Here you go. Enjoy it. You'll be back on RAF dog rations later, and I'll bet they don't taste anything close to this!'

The lump of burger was visible for a second before Buster wolfed it down. He looked at me. It was the look I had been hoping for since we left Scotland. We had connected thanks to the power of fast food, and it felt good. I savoured the comforting noise of Buster licking his lips the rest of the way.

I'm sure he was missing Nick, but by the time we reached Waddo there was only just enough time to take him for a short run before settling him into his new kennel. 'Hey Buster, you OK lad?' I asked, just before I was about to close the kennel door. He looked sad. In the circumstances, who wouldn't? I opened the door again and I knelt down and ruffled his curly coated ears and the top of his head. His nose lifted up to catch my hand and then he looked me dead in the eye and I told him, 'You're going to be OK, you know that, and we're going to be mates. I'll look after you and you look after me, that's the way it goes.'

If anyone says to me that dogs can't talk I will argue till I'm blue in the face that they certainly can. I swear that in just one look Buster told me that I had better not turn out to be an arrogant arse, otherwise he would have to teach me a lesson. I wasn't going to challenge him, after all this was a dog with campaign medals all of his own. I had high hopes for tomorrow – day one of our five weeks' training before deploying to Afghanistan.

CHAPTER 2

Playtime is Over

The next morning I woke with a schoolboy excitement. I had a new dog to play with and it felt like Christmas morning. Of course I couldn't be sure that Buster would be feeling the same sense of joy. At three years old, Buster was onto his third handler and, as a military working dog, he could quite feasibly have another three or four people to call master before his retirement in around four years' time.

When I reached Buster, he was pacing and every now and again looking up to see who was coming. He recognised me immediately and bounded up to the kennel door to take a closer look. He gave me a very cool once-over and then threw me what I can only describe as another frown. I got the distinct feeling that, in the bright light of a new day, he was slightly under-impressed with what stood before him. Not to worry, onwards and upwards, and besides I had another piece of bribery that was bound to cement our friendship – this time proper dog treats.

'Sit. Wait. Go!' I was right. The first treat disappeared without a trace. I'm not sure if the treat had the casting vote but, whatever it was, Buster was soon a very changed dog. He was round my legs as if they were covered in sirloin steaks. Bouncy, happy, ready for his walk, his breakfast and a bit of grooming. Nick was right, this dog did know all the ropes and all the tricks and he was only three years old! I wondered how many others he had fooled with his 'I'm so upset' act, before holding them to ransom for a tasty treat. Clever bugger!

This happy version of Buster was more like the dog I wanted to spend the next six months with. Who I could imagine sharing my most intimate and fear-ridden moments with in our darkest hours. A part of me admired Buster for seeing right through me and holding out for the food.

Trotting happily at my heels he could have been out on a country walk with his new master, and not a care in the world. He looked confident and I was pleased, but this was the moment of truth: if I let him off his lead, would he stay or would he run like the wind? Waddo, like most airfields, is home to a million rabbits and so far that morning they must have wondered why the new recruit wasn't giving them the expected runaround. On the lead, Buster didn't even give them a second look and for me that was a big positive. If free-running rabbits didn't bother him at home he was less likely to be distracted by all the tempting sights and smells in Afghanistan.

'Well done Buster, nice work. But if you run now I promise I will be right on your tail mate and don't think I'm joking.' I slipped the lead off his collar and we carried on walking. Within a few feet Buster realised that he was 'free' and for one heart-stopping moment I watched him bolt towards the perimeter fence.

'Don't do it! Don't make me look a prat chasing my dog over an entire airfield. Please. There's a good dog, there's a handsome spaniel ... there goes my dignity ...' I could hear myself chant the words over and over like a spell, as I watched Buster swagger his way into the distance.

Then suddenly, without any trigger, he turned tail and headed back towards me. 'Thank God ... you marvellous dog ... I knew you wouldn't do that to me ... you good fella ...' Pushing his snout at my legs he took a moment to check the 'treat pocket'. Then, when he found it empty, he dashed away again.

I started to wonder if our relationship was going to be based on my ability to produce food at the drop of a hat: this wasn't going to be and can never be the case with a working dog. Those big, soft brown eyes were hard to resist and his begging act was worthy of an Oscar, but after twenty-three years working with dogs, I had seen it all before and it just wasn't going to wash. An Arms and Explosives Search (AES) dog like Buster is trained to search, and when he locates a 'find' his reward is a tennis ball. If he finds, *then* he plays. Food does not come into any part of training or working.

I could tell this was one savvy spaniel, wise beyond his years, who could take human tolerance to its limit. On the other hand, he didn't suffer fools gladly: I was grateful that he made an exception for me.

*

I needed to see what Buster was made of. As soon as he saw the harness he knew that our playtime was over. I was pleased to see the switch to work mode was instant, and Buster knew that it would be that way until the harness was removed. Bright-eyed and alert to my instructions, Buster sat waiting patiently for me to tell him what to do.

Our training would comprise a series of route marches in full kit, live-firing, battlefield inoculation (awareness of gunfire and explosions), field craft (environment awareness training for the handler) and, for dogs like Buster, training in how to recognise the latest intelligence in the search for the weapons and explosives being used in Afghanistan at that time.

That first morning, I decided to put him to the test with two searches; the first one was set out indoors where it is easier to control the environment and the dog. A training sample of explosives was hidden in the sergeant's mess. Nose in the air, his body weaving, Buster found it in record time. He did the same with the test outdoors.

As our training continued I realised it was true. Buster was every inch the expert search dog I'd heard so much about. For a start his pace was strikingly methodical and super-steady, which meant he didn't expend too much energy as he worked. This would be vital in the extreme heat in Afghan – what we all called Afganistan for short. But more than this, he was faultless – in all the trials he located every test 'find', going straight to the hidden arms and explosives. He was amazing and I told him so several times a day.

He was a cut above any dog I had worked with before.

During our training together I learned a lot from Buster. I found myself not just working with him but feeling in awe of him too. One of the most important parts of any dog training is: don't take yourself too seriously. To be honest, sometimes I felt I was working with another person, not a dog at all. It was like the definite switch in attitude that you see in a fellow airman: one minute all jokes and blokey banter down the pub and the next total focus, weapon in hand and ready to serve and protect for Queen and country.

He had this uncanny knack of not just detecting explosives but detecting when you needed cheering up too. Just when I was in danger of getting lost in thoughts about Afghanistan, Buster would come and lean against me to offer a bit of comfort or give me a big nudge with his wet chocolate snout. In seconds I found myself fussing him and chatting to him and the moment of angst passed – thanks to Buster.

One thing that made me laugh from the start was Buster's 'indication' – how he told me and the rest of the team that he had located a 'find'. Most dogs trained for this work will sit or stand to indicate, but Buster did something else entirely – he performed a little jig with his front paws and growled! I laughed the first time I saw it, in fact it made me chuckle every time. He looked so intense and so funny all at the same time. But the hugely serious side to Buster's little 'dance' was that when he did it there was, without a shadow of a doubt, a weapon or explosives right under his nose. With Buster, there was no mistake.

After the five weeks of Buster taking me through my paces, we were both ticking all the boxes for deployment. Buster had completed all his tests and, thanks to him being the task master that he was, I felt I pushed myself harder too.

Now we were just down to the paperwork.

Making your last will and testament is something a lot of people in Civvy Street put off day after day, year after year. After all, who wants to think about dying when you're so busy living? The Armed Forces take a different view. If you sign up to give your life for your country it's as well to assume that you could end up doing exactly that. Making and writing goodbye letters is all part of the job, but one of the hardest things that you ever have to do.

'Hey Buster, you OK lad?' I remember saying, just before I closed the kennel door one evening. I knelt down and ruffled his long curly-coated ears until he closed his eyes and leaned back into a mini-trance. Buster had spent the past two hours settled on my feet as I wound up the paperwork the RAF needed me to complete before we boarded the Helmand Taxi in the morning. Somehow it was easier to write my last will and testament with the weight of a spaniel on my legs.

I wrote to my mum and dad, brother and sister, and to my wife Tracy who was deployed in Iraq. I told them all I thought they would need to know if this was a one-way ticket to Afghanistan. Buster was quiet. By the time I had finished my paperwork he was lying full-length on my body, all four feet in the air, his head on my thighs and his lips dropped back displaying a rather impressive set of teeth. Like a hairy comfort blanket he stayed with me for the whole time. And as I wrote I looked down at Buster who was snoring and flinching in his sleep. I didn't realise until I read my letters back that I had written quite a lot about the hairy fella.

Everyone who knows me knows that I am a dog lover, but in case the letters did turn out to be the last thing I ever penned, I wanted to make sure that my family were well aware of how this dog – in five short weeks – had found his way into my heart. He was now going to be my closest companion in the most dangerous place on God's earth. My loved ones needed to know that I trusted him with my life because that's the level of trust that can save you out there. The thing is, I would have needed an entire ream of paper to express my true feeling for this clever bloody spaniel.

'You know something Buster? Tracy's going to want to see us both home safe and sound. Like I've told you before, you're going to be OK and we'll be mates through whatever shit hits the fan out there. Remember, I'll look after you and you look after me.' It didn't matter that my legs were completely numb, it was good to have him there when I was preparing my goodbyes to everything and everyone I knew.

As I wandered Buster back to the kennel block, I wondered if he could possibly sense what lay ahead. I was sure he could. Everyone's behaviour patterns were different, and Buster was quieter too. Like a pet who sees the suitcases stacked in the hall at home, he must have sensed we were on the move. I think he was trying to tell me not to worry because as we walked side by side he changed his gait every now and then and nudged into me. I don't know if he needed to be tactile or he sensed that I needed something from him, but it worked anyway.

Buster didn't argue about going into his bed. He padded around a few times and then dropped into a neat curl, head on paws and one ear spread over the floor in a very neat swirl. I gave him a pat and then tiptoed away so the crunch of my big boots on the kennel floor wouldn't disturb him. I closed the door and looked back. Buster's head was down, but his eyes were wide open.

CHAPTER 3

Desert Dog

I didn't sleep much that night. By the look of Buster when I went to 'wake' him, he had had a rough night too. 'Come on mate, let's make sure you have a bit of breakfast before we have to jump on the plane. No one wants to see you when you're hungry. A walk, a bit of scoff and a quick brush-up will get you right. I'm hoping it will work for me too.'

Buster looked as enthusiastic as I did about the whole thing. He plodded next to me as we headed to the kennel door where he took a big breath of morning air and sprung out to meet the dew.

Refreshed by his 'shower', Buster was ready for his breakfast. For now this would be the usual military working dog diet of dry and wet mix, but he would soon be sharing food with me – boil-in-the-bag style. I had packed a few extra pouches for him along with everything else, from grooming brush to water bottle to working harness. He tried to help me pack the night before by lying all over the gear I had laid out on the section floor. Just the kind of help you need when you're packing for deployment – a sprawling, attention seeking spaniel. After being moved off the kit, he'd sat and watched me the whole time. His muscular liver-and-white body sat solid and square. His silky head held high and chocolate coloured nose in the air. In one statement of body language he said to me: 'Come on. Man up.'

I'd told him what we were about to embark on, the most dangerous episode of our lives, and that he had to be a good dog and do his job. I remember how unimpressed he looked. He was a search dog with a list of credits to his name, and to him this was just another jolly with a few new friends. I was the idiot. And it was clear to Buster that I was a scared idiot at that.

By the time the dog van arrived to take us to RAF Brize Norton, where we would fly out, I realised there was no turning back. It was September 2007, and we were in for a six-month tour. As long as Buster got through his licensing and was passed fit to go on duty, we would be on the ground in days. I already knew that we would be in demand. Throughout the five weeks' training and the additional time spent concentrating on practise searches it was clear there was a huge shortage of dog handlers. The Royal Army Veterinary Corps handlers were under pressure – with all units wanting a dog to work alongside them, and not enough to go round. I had no idea who we would be assigned to, but I knew Buster would work his heart out for them.

For some reason I couldn't shift a nugget of fear that had planted itself in my head the night before, while packing and writing the letters. Thankfully there was lots of banter to be had with the driver, who was an old friend of mine, and that helped pass the couple of hours' motorway drive to Brize.

The huge C-17 transport aircraft was waiting for us. By the time we had got through all the usual security on the gate and produced all the right papers it was time to head for the plane. I took comfort from the sight of Buster swaggering along as if he was heading for a walk in the park. I realised that Buster had it all right and I had it all wrong: I immediately took a leaf from his book and picked up my spirits. After all, this is what I joined up to do, and let's face it, I wasn't alone. As we walked, Buster checked back on me every now and again. I took that look to be spaniel 'speak' for, 'Well come on fat boy, pick up your feet. The plane won't wait for us two you know.'

The C-17 was dark and cavernous, like I imagine the belly of a whale to be. It looked as if it was filled with random items from RAF stores, including a Lynx helicopter which was parked in one corner. Apart from the three-man crew of pilot, co-pilot and loadmaster, there was just me and Buster, plus Corporal Mike Mortimer and his German shepherd Patrol Dog Bony, and Corporal Phil Janney with German shepherd Patrol Dog Zeus.

Mild-mannered Buster was clever enough to give not-so-mild-mannered Bony and Zeus all the personal space they needed. Dogs know dogs, and Buster got the measure of his fellow travellers pretty quickly. The German shepherds were trained protection dogs;

that's protect their handler and guard whatever they are told to. It was no secret that in a matter of seconds they could morph into snarling balls of hair and teeth if they felt the need.

Buster, I soon learned, didn't sit on the floor if he could help it. His canine companions were already in their transit kennels but checking to his right, and then left and centre, Buster quickly surveyed the seating arrangements and bagged himself the seat next to me. I wouldn't have been surprised if he had chosen to spread out on a row all to himself. However, it wasn't to be and into a transit kennel he had to go. The look I got was less than impressed. 'OK lad, this isn't quite what you're used to but it'll keep you safe and you won't rattle around so much as the rest of us over there.'

This was a seven-hour trip all the way to Turkey, where we would re-fuel and wait for the safety of nightfall for the flight on to Kandahar. The constant drone of the C-17 was strangely comforting and sleep came easily. I looked at the Bergan I had packed tightly with everything I could ever need for an airman and his search dog. I looked at my feet, which had disappeared into the huge RAF issue desert boots and thought how new and ridiculously clean they were. Mentally I located the bag of food treats and planned to give Buster something tasty when he woke.

We landed in Kandahar at half past midnight and artificial light suddenly powered into the aircraft.

Buster stirred and yawned. 'We're here boy,' I said, giving him a shake on his shoulders. 'Here's a little something for you to enjoy before we start the process of being here.' I offered Buster a scrap of cooked bacon, from our in-flight meal, which he took with a little nodding of his head. He stood calmly at my side while I gathered everything together to leave the aircraft for the last leg of the journey to Camp Bastion.

The transfer was going smoothly for everyone except Bony and Zeus, who decided to pick a fight with everyone who came near them. They weren't sure who was friend or foe, so everyone felt the force of their frustrations that night. Spitting fury from the confines of their kennels, the two big guys surged forward at Buster – who didn't flick a whisker. He sat in front of them, solid as a rock but looking past them. The wily dog was not stupid enough to make eye contact but sitting there, just out of their reach, drove them crazy. Barking and making a fuss was not Buster's way of doing things. He disapproved and he let them know by throwing them one of his super dirty looks. This was when Buster was more human than dog. His facial expressions and body language were so perfect and so eloquent that no one was left in any doubt as to how he felt.

Fortunately we didn't have to wait too long before we were ordered aboard the C-130 Hercules, the Camp Bastion 'taxi'. The giant plane was packed to capacity with a mixture of supplies and military personnel. Again, for this leg Buster had to be transferred to a transit kennel and I didn't relish explaining it to him. But as we approached the row of quite cosy looking kennels Buster seemed to know that one of them was for him. I went ahead and opened the door so he could just hop right in. He sniffed around for a few seconds, did a couple of turns, and then got himself comfortable.

I had hoped the walk we'd managed to grab before boarding would be enough to calm him for the rest of the journey, but I was the only one worrying. Buster was in sleep mode before I had finished securing the catch on the kennel door.

Full body armour, helmets, gloves and night vision goggles was the dress code for the flight into Bastion. It was no secret that the Taliban watched the comings and goings of the air traffic in and out of the base, and from the moment the plane touched down we needed to be ready for action. Flying in darkness prompted virtual silence. It gives you plenty of time to consider what the next six months could hold – sitting there with my colleagues, all of us dressed ready for battle, was a sobering experience. I leant forward to check on Buster and all was quiet inside. Bony and Zeus were still up for a challenge and seeing me cranked up the noise level. But there was no bark of discontent from Buster, who just turned a deaf ear to it all. I kept forgetting that he had done all this before when he went to Bosnia. He was not new to war, just new to me. I leant back knowing he was fine and that I was the one sweating-up, not him.

After a short while the noise of the Hercules kicking back for descent focused my mind again. Seconds later we got the call to prepare for landing in total darkness. The pull of the descent was stomach churning but it's all about timing: get the plane on the ground, unloaded, re-loaded and re-fuelled, and back in the air ASAP. The wheels bounced on the desert earth and everyone started their preparations to disembark. The belly of the plane filled with artificial light. The race against time had begun.

The noise of the landing and the commotion surrounding the unloading probably woke Buster long before I reached him. I could tell he was pleased to see me as he started his little jogging dance. I was already laden with my Bergan and extra baggage so I was able to secure Buster on his lead and head straight off the plane.

The ground staff moved swiftly to get everything off and then the next lot on board for the return journey. It was strange seeing the guys who were headed home to their loved ones. They had that faraway gaze, and looked ready for a good meal and a hot bath. Just for a second I wanted to be with them.

Then the lights went out again and we were left to watch the plane leave us for the relative safety of Kandahar.

The moment we stepped onto the sands around Camp Bastion we entered a different world from the dewy grass that Buster had last felt on his coat. The dryness of the dust hit me in the face and clung to my skin. Buster sniffed the ground as soon as we stepped from the Hercules and the sticky sand attached itself to his wet nose.

We had been told that we would be met by a member of the Royal Army Veterinary Corps dog handler team, who we were now out there to support. I guess having a dog made me pretty easy to spot in the crowd of people that had just arrived. We were met by Sergeant Al Smith, who was to be our ops sergeant for the tour. He welcomed us and piled us into the most knackered Land Rover that I have ever come across.

With the promise of a full guided tour of Bastion later on we were escorted to the Dog Section, then known as the 'Muttley Lines'. This was to be Buster's home for the next couple of days while I got to grips with RSOI (that's Reception Staging and Onward Integration). This was the final stage of briefs and refresher training on everything you could ever need to know about everything that could save your life or someone else's. I also had to check that my weapon sights were still zeroed, meaning that we could shoot straight if and when the time came. It was all pretty intense and that included the living accommodation too – two hundred of us, in bunk beds, living in one huge tent. I think Buster was probably having a better time of it.

It was a massive relief to be able to get onto the next stage, which was in-theatre training with Buster. This was the chance to translate some of that five weeks of training at Waddo into on-the-spot action in Afghan.

Buster was exposed to the latest threats being used by the enemy, but this time we were working in the relevant climate and terrain – which of course he took in his stride.

Night searches were something we were both going to have to get used to. Searching in night vision goggles was not one of my favourite things and I could sense that Buster realised this as soon as I put them on. There was no doubt he was laughing his speckly socks off as I stumbled around the place tripping over rocks and tipping into ditches. Never mind, we got the hang of it and gained our license to go out into the field.

This is when it really kicks in that you are about to do something really dangerous. Your next-of-kin details and insurance cover are checked before you are 'sanitised' – asked to hand in your ID card, bank cards, photos of loved ones and anything else that could endanger you or others if you were captured. I packed my Bergan and re-packed it several times before I was happy that I had everything and in a sensible order. I would be carrying it most of the time and it was no mean weight with Buster's stuff in there as well as mine.

As we waited for our transport to the helipad the whole site was in a state of readiness, with units preparing to be uplifted to various parts of Helmand. I was off to Forward Operating Base Price, slap bang in the middle of the Green Zone. This used to get confused with the Green Zone in Iraq, which is the area full of top hotels and restaurants. When I told people back home I was off there, they thought I was in for a cushy time. But they were wrong. This Green Zone is so called because of the vegetation fed from the mighty Helmand River. Unfortunately some of the vegetation is the opium poppy, harvested by the enemy to fund their deadly plans – which made this a critical strategic location. We were very aware that we were heading straight for the Taliban heartland.

Nevertheless, as we prepared to board the plane there was plenty of laughing and joking going on, but it was mixed with an entirely different look, one of trepidation. As we walked out to board an American Blackhawk and were surrounded by Danish as well as British soldiers, I noticed for the first time what a truly international operation this was.

Buster did what I knew would be his usual trick, and jumped onto one of the seats, much to everyone's amusement. The door gunners, looking almost space age in their futuristic-style helmets, strapped in and checked their weapons. As the Blackhawk lurched ahead we rose up and away, Bastion sprawled massively beneath us. Flying low and fast, the walls of Bastion quickly blurred and blended into the landscape, perfectly camouflaged – the camp disappeared as if it had been just a mirage.

The never-ending spread of scorched, orange earth of the Upper Gereshk Valley stretched out beneath us. We were in the air for just fifteen minutes before we touched down. The doors opened immediately.

Baggage, post bags and passengers were dumped unceremoniously onto the stony ground. As we headed off, others were alighting, many wearing that fast-becoming-familiar 'thousand-yard stare' – a stare into the distance registering nothing – a look I would see a lot more of in the months to come. Within no time the helicopter was ready to move off, the rest of us lying on our baggage and on the precious mail sacks that had arrived with us to stop it all blowing away.

Scrambling off the ground in a whirl of sand and bags, and with Buster in hand, I became concerned that this vast dust bowl of a place was going to cause breathing problems for Buster. He was going to be sniffing-up the sticky plaster-like muck while he worked, slept and ate. Huge sneezes and spluttery coughs had, so far, managed to clear Buster's airways but it was something I would be keeping a close eye on. I knew that other dogs were suffering with dust in their eyes and 'doggles' were proving to be a great success in some cases, but I am not a fan. They are a distraction that I can do without. The dog's third eyelid has served it well for thousands of years in any case.

For now our priority was to get to the Operations tent and introduce ourselves to the 2nd Battalion MERCIAN (Worcester and Foresters). I was told right away that the current handler on duty was out in the field, so I decided to check out the Dog Section. Buster had other ideas. He decided to check out the post room. It just so happened that a welfare parcel had just arrived addressed to 'A Dog in Afghanistan'.

It happened daily, along with parcels marked 'For a Soldier in Afghanistan'. These are well-meaning and welcome gifts from members of the public that contain generous helpings of sweet treats and toiletries, books and sometimes gadgets such as iPods for the soldiers. For the dogs, they contained their body weight in chews and toys. Buster immediately made friends with the girls in the post room and landed himself the biggest dog chew I had ever seen.

After getting Buster's new friends to promise me that they wouldn't give in to his big brown eyes every time, we wandered off to the kennels. Spacious and air-conditioned, the dog accommodation was pretty good and there was a 'sitting room' area with tables and chairs crafted out of crates and pallets, where dogs and handlers could relax their way. I noticed there was a note on the table from a colleague, pointing me in the direction of the store containing all the food, training samples and everything dog handlers love to hoard. That was a secret I would not be sharing with Buster. I decided to give Buster his meal and we settled down, me reading a book and him having a post-supper snooze at my feet.

When I called into the Ops tent later for a briefing there was a massive buzz with the news that some of our troops were engaged in fighting just a few miles away. Now we knew we'd arrived. I listened intently as the reports of the TIC (Troops In Contact) came in. I realised that this was very real. I could only pray that we had trained hard enough for the challenges to come.

CHAPTER 4

Buster's New Friends

It wasn't long before we got our first taste of combat. Just a few days later we were holed up deep in the belly of a Viking armoured vehicle, as the Taliban took shots at us as we sped through the dusty desert valleys. The sound of the bullets striking the truck still rang in my ears as our driver took us clear of the ambush. As I reassured the team about Buster's safety – 'all good with the dog' – which was always a priority for the crew, our convoy of Vikings crossed over the Helmand River and once again headed into the desert. My fellow soldiers were still bemoaning the enemy's lucky escape, but we had a job to do.

The heat had not yet entered the day. Nevertheless, it was a long rough ride in a vehicle clearly built for practicality not comfort. The stench of diesel and weapon oil was snatching at my throat. The gloom was gradually giving way to a golden morning and I could see a clear silhouette of Buster's head, which he had pushed right up to the small slit window in the back door. There was little to see out there except for the long line of Vikings. Every now and then we would catch sight of an Afghan community, the low, yellow buildings trailing, and then there was nothing to see again for miles.

But then we reached the outskirts of Gereshk, and the scenery changed. There were clusters of buildings: all squat mud walls that looked as if they were falling down. As we slowed to pass through a market place, I saw several of the local people just sitting, staring at us with suspicious glares. Buster started to wag his tail and pad his front feet up and down in excitement, pleased at the good turnout he imagined he had attracted.

Eventually the convoy came to a screeching halt, and the huge panelled door on the back of our Viking was opened from the outside. We stepped out into the bright sunlight. The gunner took the opportunity to check the vehicle for damage: 'Not a mark on her sir,' he reported, giving the Viking a pat on the side. 'They might as well have been hurling balls of wet cotton wool at us. Bastards!'

We had reached the checkpoint just ahead of the compound where we would be staying for the next couple of weeks. All around us soldiers were milling around in various states of morning undress and this was just what Buster needed – a new audience.

First, after several waking and sleeping hours spent in the confines of the Viking, the moment called for a good long dog stretch: forwards, making his feathery hind legs look exceptionally long and then backwards resting almost completely on his haunches to extend his front legs. All this accompanied by a jaw breaking yawn. Happier, Buster skipped over to the guys whose faces lit up at the slightly bizarre sight of an English springer spaniel sniffing and rooting around in the Afghan sand. It's just what he would do on a walk back home but this time it was with a huge patch of sand on his nose instead of sweet black earth. The guys' expressions were priceless: delight, laughter and open arms welcomed Buster, who was now in super-sniff mode checking people's pockets.

'So what's your name then fella? Come here; let's have a look at you. So you're our new bomb dog are you?' said a young soldier, no more than twenty years old, who was kneeling down and cradling Buster's head in his hands. 'Well we'd better look after you then. Hey, any of you lot got a treat for our new dog?'

I noticed a wave of activity as the guys rifled their pockets and checked through their kit, and produced bits of biscuit and sweet leftovers from the latest food parcel a girlfriend, wife or mother had sent with love from home. I could see that a lot of the guys were falling for Buster's well-rehearsed 'I'm absolutely STARVING!' look. I watched him working his crowd. The big, sad brown eyes and the silky head leaning to one side, followed by the raised paw and every move delivered with perfect timing.

'OK, that's enough of that you old fraud. Nice try.' I must have sounded like an old misery guts and even Buster threw me a look that said, 'What? Come on Dad ... give a dog a break!'

Mr 'I'm not happy with you but I know I've got to do as I'm told' started to trot towards me. His brows were down and his ears were heading in the same direction, but I knew if I left Buster in the hands of these guys he would be as big as a barrel in no time at all. To them my dog was a bit of normality amid the craziness. But in less than twenty-four hours Buster would be with these men patrolling the tracks and compounds of the Upper Gereshk Valley – their lives depending on him. He could have treats every now and again, but I didn't want him to get settled as there would soon be work to do.

While Buster made one last attempt to soak up the adoration from his new friends I took a look around. The base where the Viking had dropped us probably measured a cosy 200 by 10 metres. It was surrounded by Hesco Bastion (collapsible, sand-filled wire mesh barriers) and furnished with an eclectic mix of small shelters handmade by the troops for an extra touch of home comfort – to protect from the glare of the extreme heat during the day and the icy cold contrast of the desert nights. Just beyond all of this was a bridge over the Helmand River.

Like the fairground rides that disappear like magic overnight, the Vikings vanished into the desert. Then a quad bike arrived in a cloud of dust and, almost without stopping, the rider dismounted and introduced himself as the squadron quartermaster for A Company 2nd Battalion MERCIAN. In one sweep of a burnished brown arm he loaded my kit onto a trailer and set off for the main camp, 600 metres away. We were joined by eight young soldiers and made our way to the compound, known as The Fan.

The compound was split into two by a large wall. I took Buster on a walk round. On one side was a building that was the main house turned into a military headquarters. Close to this there was a well for water and a smaller outbuilding which was being used by the interpreters. The rest of the compound was divided by Hesco Bastion into small living areas and over the wall from there spread a car park that would later be filled by the returning Vikings.

At each corner of the compound watchtowers had been hastily erected by the Royal Engineers and were now manned by some of the young soldiers we had met when we arrived.

'Hi Buster, how are you doing mate?' It was the same young man who had knelt with Buster earlier. 'You're welcome here any time you like, you hear me?'

I'm convinced Buster recognised the lad and understood the open invitation to come visit any time he liked. It didn't take the wily spaniel long to discover that the watchtowers were the coolest place in the compound and I knew that if he went missing he would be there with the blokes on sentry duty, just to get a waft of cool breeze through his fur.

After a gruelling morning keeping busy filling sandbags, I moved into one of the segregated areas and got out my mosquito pod, or 'mozzipod' as they are better known. Without a scrap of confidence I started to assemble it but soon realised that the two-by-one-metre tarpaulin base, covered with one metre tall mesh was clearly out to confuse me. Buster slumped onto the ground, put his head down between his paws and sighed, deeply. He probably gathered from my puzzled expression that this was going to take a while.

As I crouched over the instructions praying for inspiration, a colossus of a man appeared and cast a huge shadow that woke Buster from his nap. He was one of the Royal Marines Vikings. 'Can I give your dog a pig's ear?' he asked.

It took me a bit by surprise. After all I can't say it was a question I was expecting to answer anytime at all in the Afghan desert. 'Yes mate, no worries,' I replied, and Buster gratefully received the gift with a huge spaniel smile.

It hit me just how much dogs mean to people so far away from home. Buster was there as a bomb dog, not a pet, but it didn't matter. At no time would a Royal Marine's official kit list read: weapon, ammunition, water, food, spare clothing and ... pigs' ears – but today it did! Our gentle giant with the secret supply of dog treats chatted for some time about dogs loved and lost in a time and place before both of us found ourselves fighting a war in the Afghan desert.

'One of you put up the sergeant's pod!' The call went out from Lance Corporal 'Chan' Chandler, who must have noticed I was fighting a losing battle with the mozzipod instructions. Chan had nothing to him, having been out there so long. He had a shock of blond hair, well bleached by the sun, and always had a smile on his face – except when describing past battles. Chan (later to be Mentioned in Dispatches for his unstinting devotion to his men) was a man I came to respect in a very short space of time. The mozzipod was quickly assembled for me, much to my embarrassment, but at least I could rest easy knowing Buster and I had a bed for the night.

Chan was eager to take the opportunity to introduce me to some of the lads – so many fantastic and inspiring young people. Some who Buster would become particularly fond of were Mac, a lance corporal who would later be Mentioned in Dispatches; Chrissie, one of twins in the same company; Carling, who had a song about just about any subject; and Sergeant Michael 'Locky' Lockett. Locky was to be the first person to receive the Military Cross since World War II, and was tragically killed on his third tour of Afghanistan a couple of years later. Yet, truth be told, Buster made friends with everyone, whether they liked it or not. He was that kind of dog.

As I settled into the camp, Chan told me that just a couple of days before Buster and I arrived, the unit had been involved in a massive engagement that had claimed the lives of two of their men.

'It wasn't supposed to go like that,' said Chan. 'It was a pre-planned operation to disrupt the Taliban, but the attack on our blokes was ferocious. A sergeant lost his life and when we reached his colleague he was still clinging to his light machine gun and it was still in fire position. He died making sure that his comrades could get away.'

I'm not sure if Chan had noticed or been conscious of it at all, but as we were talking Buster had appeared, sniffed my hand and settled beside me. Then I saw him check out the situation. It took him less than a second to work out who needed him most. He threw one last look at me, as if to ask my permission: 'You OK with this Dad? It's just where I need to be right now. OK?' I nodded to him and right away he settled by Chan's side.

'I've seen some stuff out here and I can never forget it.'

As Chan was describing the horror of finding his comrades dead, he stabbed the air with his clenched fists and suddenly one hand fell hard on Buster. It was unintentional and Buster didn't flinch. All the time Chan was talking Buster lay still and allowed the lance corporal to stroke him. I think it was good for Chan to unburden himself to an outsider, but to have Buster sitting by him soaking up the emotion and allowing his ears to be stroked was, I could see, a great comfort. I don't think I'd ever seen a dog do that so honestly before.

There are no set mealtimes when you're in the desert: you eat when you are hungry. Rather than everyone lighting their own 'hexi' stoves it made sense to some of the guys to fashion just one central fire pit out of bricks and have a big pot of water steaming away on it all the time. That way, whenever you were hungry, you just dropped your boil-in-the-bag banquet in to cook.

Ration packs – or 'rat' packs as we called them – come in two kinds: ten-man and individual twenty-four hour. We were on individual ones. I can tell you for certain that ration packs have improved tremendously in the last two decades. In the past they were pure stodge designed to fill you up and keep you going. Now they are scientifically formulated to provide a nutritional balance suited to fighting troops on the move. To Buster they were just food. Having said that, anyone eating the all-day breakfast flavour would soon learn that each pouch came with a determined springer spaniel attached.

I quickly worked out that swapping food was the norm out there. I was in the enviable position of having a Bergan full of sweets and biscuits courtesy of my stay at FOB Price. Someone had given me good advice while I was at Bastion, and that was when you push forward to a new location to load up with treats for the lads that are out on the ground, they would be forever grateful. I had bought several bags of sweets but I was also offered extras by Buster's friends in the post room. They had several boxes addressed to 'A Soldier in Afghanistan' that they wanted distributing, I had opened the boxes and taken out the sweets, biscuits and toiletries and packed them into my Bergan for the lads.

After everyone had had their ration pack and it had reached that time when everyone was searching for something sweet, I decided it was the right time to share the spoils. Much to Buster's disgust I started to hand them out right under his wet, twitching nose. His toes started to dance; he looked agitated and scampered into a central position so he could watch every move I made. Buster's head flinched and his ears swished from side to side as he flung himself around to follow my hands as the treats shifted around the group of guys. No sooner had all been gratefully received than Buster swirled into action – to retrieve the food!

The lads of 2 MERCIAN were coming to the end of their six-month tour. The signs of battle fatigue were massively evident on their faces. As Buster padded around, every now and then one of the men would reach out and encourage Buster to come to them and the next second they would be talking to him and hugging him. Buster was proving to be a good listener and absorbed the odd tear or two along the way. You can do that with a dog.

Within hours Buster and I felt we had been with the guys for weeks, and it was good to see Buster lifting the men's spirits just by being around them.

I was starting to feel a real bond with this dog.

When we got back to our section of the compound we discovered that Chan had ordered a gate to be fashioned so that Buster could stay with us without being tethered. Carling had been very creative with Hesco panels and made a lovely 'frame' that was to become Buster's new temporary home. Like a proud new home owner Buster looked around the new facilities and gave it his sniff of approval. 'What about this then old lad? You're here five minutes and you've already got folk doing things for you. You're like royalty or something. Come here!' Buster ran into my arms and we had a good old wrestle – until something caught his eye. The men were on the move. Playtime was over.

An officer in charge of the Intelligence Section introduced himself. 'We're off to the poppy fields. Local intelligence sources have indicated insurgent activity so Buster will be heading up our patrol. Word is we'll be looking for hidden weapons.'

Buster would lead the patrol and locate any dangers in our path. There was an up and coming new danger, the IED (Improvised Explosive Device) – a hidden, silent threat, lurking in the ground and a favourite of the Taliban. I knew that if anything was there, Buster would find it.

My dog was ready to get going but, according to the squadron quartermaster, I wasn't. He asked me how much ammunition I had and when I told him, he laughed and then handed me a more realistic supply, which included high explosive grenades and red phosphorous grenades.

My God, I didn't know which was the most overwhelming feeling: the rush of steaming adrenaline, the over-powering heat, the sheer fear or the weird excitement. One thing I didn't have to worry about was Buster, who was sitting waiting for me to sort myself out. He was panting like crazy and eager to start work, and the unit was ready to move out.

There were ten of us, including two from Intelligence, and we were all carrying enough supplies to last a full twenty-four hours. Although we only expected to be out for a couple of hours, we all carried a full day's supplies just in case anything went wrong. We only had the local intelligence report to go on but if there was activity in the fields we were going to be walking right into it. We waited at the entrance to the compound, weapons cocked, ready to meet whatever was waiting for us. Sweat rolled down my face and soaked my entire body.

The patrol was 'switched on' – eyes and rifles pointed in every direction. Our interpreter ordered the local people to stay away from the patrol and, as if that wasn't enough to make them anxious, they looked pretty confused to see Buster trotting along beside us. A dog walking alongside people is pretty much an alien concept over there. The Afghan people don't regard dogs as 'companion' animals in the way we do. To them dogs are just dogs; strays, pests, good only for fighting and keeping as vicious guards.

Buster was a military working dog with a job to do, but we still saw him as a companion, a soldier even, so entitled to share our space. It was a massive culture shock for many of our servicemen and women to see dogs treated in such a different way in Afghanistan. It's probably one of the reasons why Buster got all the extra treats and hugs, because he's one dog we could reach out to.

At this time, there was little or no chance of detecting an Improvised Explosive Device (IED) buried in the ground. It wasn't the norm then to have soldiers walking ahead with metal detectors. I checked Buster's harness again, probably the fifth time I'd done that since I put it on him at the base. A working dog wearing a harness is like me putting on my uniform, a sign that he is on duty and it's the best way for me to say to him: 'That's it now, no more arsing around, we've got work to do.' It works every time. A high visibility harness is the normal kit for a working dog, a bit like a canine 'safety' jacket, but the last thing I wanted was Buster to become a fluorescent beacon for Taliban snipers – a dead dog walking. Instead he was wearing plain black, which, in my mind, is the safest uniform for a bomb dog in Afghanistan.

Buster lifted his head to catch what little air he could from the stifling heat. 'Sorry mate,' I said, 'I know it's not the best place to be wearing a fur coat but we'll take this at your pace and we'll be OK.'

He looked at me as if to say: 'That's fine. Now can we just get on with it?' He was right and his legs stretched and flexed like a coiled spring. Anyone watching would see that I was the jumpy one out of the two of us, and as I surveyed the search area I can tell you it looked like no field you would see in the UK.

The September fields lay stripped of their beautiful but deadly opium harvest. The closest comparison I can think of is wheat fields after harvest, when the stubble has been burned black right down to the earth. But the Afghan fields are grown in sand instead of soil and, without the beauty of the bright red poppy petals, all that remains is the browned husks and the long black stems of the dying plants. Several local young FAMs (what we term 'fighting age males') were hanging around the fields, which would be commonplace during the harvest when they do the bulk of the work, but they only made themselves conspicuous being there when it was all over.

'OK Buster, time to go.' He had been ready to go for ages and I had seen him cast his eyes over the ground as soon as we arrived. Alert, fine-boned, head held high, Buster looked ahead, a short check back to me and then moved forward, nose in the air, tail wagging as he took in the scents in true springer fashion. I knew that if there were any weapons or explosives hidden in the ground we were about to walk on, Buster would find them first. Walking carefully, a good distance behind him, I watched the master at work weaving and swaggering his way over the ground.

At that moment in time I'm sure Buster was the only one with a cool head and dry body. The rest of the patrol was watching me and more than that they were watching Buster's every move. But then, 'Sergeant, call your dog in. We have a suspect in for questioning and if we don't get out of here right now we're going to be the next target for the Taliban. They will be looking for revenge and any of us will do.'

I'm not sure if my heart stopped or just leaped, but our patrol leader's order brought the search to an abrupt halt. Buster takes his orders from me and as I opened my mouth to call him back I couldn't help smiling at the dear dog as he carried on sniffing away in search of his 'prize'.

Dusty chocolate nose off the ground, Buster looked to me as if to say: 'Oh, but I've only just started! Come on; let me carry on ... please?' The cute tail wagging and puppy dog eyes wasn't going to work this time. It was definitely time to go.

'Buster get your arse back here!' It must have been the tone of my voice that put Buster into reverse. He dropped the crazy tail wagging and carefully picked his way back towards me using the tracks he had made in the sand. 'Come on you, let's go and find out what's going on,' I said, knowing that coming away from the search area like that, without a 'find', was Buster's idea of unfair play. He's doing the job to earn a few minutes downtime playing with his tennis ball and now I was the greatest spoilsport in the history of the world.

I left Buster in his harness just in case we were diverted elsewhere with the patrol. All we knew was that a young local man had been brought in for questioning based on information received. For the local people who understood and appreciated that our purpose was to protect their lives and livelihood, there was merit in informing on the Taliban, but it was a brave move with grave consequences if ever traced back to them.

Heading back to the compound we heard that an arrest had been made. No one needed to tell us that we had to move, now. The arrest had put a price on the head of every serviceman and woman on the road – every friend that guy had would now be out looking to get him back or seek payback.

We were approximately forty minutes away from The Fan. Walking back, everyone was on high alert – only the sound of Buster's panting filling the silence. I was thinking how this was going to feel like the longest journey ever when we suddenly came to a halt. It was Buster's cue to step up and get searching the road and the perimeter of a yellow stone wall that was causing concern up ahead. He was ready and waiting to get on with it. If there was a moment not to take my helmet off, even for a second, it was now, so I tried dipping it forward and released four huge drops of sweat, which ran down my nose and splashed onto Buster's head in quick succession. He wasn't impressed. He looked up at me, his snout wrinkled. 'Sorry mate,' I said, although the drops instantly dried to nothing.

You could almost hear nerves stretching and all eyes were on Buster. Still, patient and alert, and without doubt the coolest customer in this crisis, the only thing holding him back for my order to search was the discipline that had been drummed into him from day one of his basic training.

Buster padded the ground, looked at me, tongue lolling out of his mouth, his eyes urging me to give him the go-ahead. Half a second later he was steadily sweeping the earth: His nose working overtime, his body moves all deliberate, precise and measured, like a fully-wound clockwork toy. As he approached the corner of the yellow stone wall that was causing concern, Buster stopped. I knew this wasn't Buster's signal that he had found something – he dances and growls when that happens – but there was a sharp intake of breath from the guys. It's a kind of madness to assume that there are hidden dangers everywhere, but in a place where there are no rules it's the kind of madness that can save your life.

When he was satisfied that it was safe to move on, Buster came back to me and was able to collect a great big hug and lots of praise before we headed off safely along the road that ran past the yellow wall. It was nerve wracking watching him go forward because he faced the same risks we did. But his skills saved him as much as the rest of us.

We made one more stop along the way. Buster seemed a little reluctant this time. I couldn't see why and it bothered me that he was holding back. 'You OK, Buster? What's wrong mate?' I asked him. At the same time I could feel my heart leap in my chest. I trusted my dog's judgement and I waited for his next move. I've no idea what caused him to hesitate but he suddenly whirled into action. I think the entire patrol breathed a sigh of relief. I certainly did. Once again he signalled the road ahead was safe.

When we reached The Fan the guys fussed around Buster and he bathed in the attention before selecting a spot to sit and watch the rest of us unload our weapons. Until then, I hadn't realised just how uncomfortable I was. My combats were dark, sodden with sweat, and I couldn't blame it all on the heat, as the heart-pounding intensity of the search had taken its toll on my stress levels. I knew I had to get used to it and this was only just the start.

We were all more than ready for dinner. Buster was keen to see what was on the menu and I could see – again – that I needed to lay down a few ground rules about treats. The lads were quick to succumb to Buster's big brown eyes and would have gladly given him their entire meal. 'It's only one biscuit,' they'd say. 'Yes, but if everyone gives him "just one biscuit", he'll soon be fat and useless.' I know they understood what I was saying but I still felt a bit mean. Thankfully the lads were very good after that and always asked if they could give Buster a treat, or at least when I was around. I dread to think how many 'unauthorised' treats were given out when Buster really worked his audience. Good job his work kept him lean. Once we had finished eating I gave Buster his own meal, which he rapidly ate before foraging for leftovers.

After food I sat chatting with the lads, getting to know them and what they had been through. As a Senior NCO (non-commissioned officer), I am used to dealing with problems that my younger airmen and women bring to me, everything from debt to relationship issues and all sorts in between. But nothing could prepare me for what these young men were telling me. Only a few days into joining their desert life, I could at that time only imagine what it must be like to be sharing a laugh and a joke with your mates one minute, fighting for your life beside them the next, and then sending one of them home in a body bag.

Too soon, I was called away to join the section commanders for the evening O Group. After our day in the desert I was keen to find out the orders for the following day and try and get my head around it. I left Buster with the lads who had strict instructions about not feeding him or letting him play with stones. He has a thing about stones and the last thing I wanted to happen now was for him to end up in the vet hospital at Bastion. During Orders it was confirmed that I would be taking Buster out on foot patrol with Locky's section in the morning. Another dangerous mission lay ahead.

I finished the evening by taking Buster for his night-time stroll around the compound. What should have been taken about twenty minutes took a good hour, with Buster getting a hero's welcome from everyone – even though he hadn't found anything yet. Maybe it was more to do with knowing that he would protect them when they needed him most. More than likely it was because he was a dog and a reminder of home and normality. Whatever he meant to the lads was up to them. Buster was able to reassure the patrols we were assigned to, but it wasn't just the MERCIANs who wanted to wish him a good sleep, everyone wanted to say goodnight to the new bomb dog.

Out in the desert, once it goes dark, there isn't a lot to do. After Orders, as long as the kit is prepped for the morning, it's time for bed. Out come the iPods, red filters get attached to your head torch and it's time to settle down. As I looked around I noticed something I thought strange. The troops around me had been out in the desert in the height of summer when temperatures soar into the 50s, so they were donning their softie jackets before getting into their sleeping bags. Being freshly arrived from home I was still sweating in my T-shirt.

Buster climbed into the mozzipod and I zipped it up. Then began what was to become a nightly disagreement – who was sleeping where? This was not a good game in such a confined space. Let's put it this way, mozzis are not designed for bulky airmen and stubborn spaniels to sleep in harmony. 'For goodness' sake Buster, what on earth are you trying to do?' Buster on my head, on my chest, on my head again. 'Will you please settle down?' In true spaniel fashion Buster circled and circled as if chasing his tail while treading all over my body and just before he dropped his bottom I shifted his bulk off my groin and onto my legs. Eventually, after several leg spasms, we settled for Buster sleeping on my feet.

While reading my book and listening to my music, the song 'Forever Young' by Alphaville came on. The words are so poignant and they fixed in my head. From then on I felt the need to play it every night, if I could, and to this day when I hear it I'm transported back to that time and place. The song reminds me how beautiful the outside world looks through the skin of a mozzipod. It's amazing how clear the sky is with no pollution to cloud the view. Through the beam of my head torch I could see the dust moving about, and I wondered just what I was breathing in. Buster was fast asleep wondering nothing at all. Every now and again he kicked out a back leg as if he was running somewhere and where his lips had fallen back over his teeth, his whiskers twitched in time with his 'running'. I couldn't help smiling at the old lad. I wanted to reach out and stroke him but he was settled and happy so the last thing I wanted to do was wake him to start a new game of who's sleeping where!

All was peaceful until I heard a blast of machine gun fire in the distance. Then some controlled bursts (ours or the Danes') and then several wild, long bursts (the enemy's). Chan had explained that B Company were deployed on the banks of the Helmand River and were constantly engaged with the enemy at nightfall. This was new to me, but all around I could hear the sounds of snoring, including from Buster.

The rumbling activity had got my adrenaline flowing but eventually I must have nodded off. I've no idea how long that lasted but I woke wanting to go to the toilet and, being so quiet, it seemed like a good time to go. The toilet, aka a plank with three holes cut into it and the urinals being lengths of pipe to pee in, was crude but functional. And it was fine until it was full – in the blindness of one dead of night I was to make the grim discovery that it was overflowing onto my feet. Not that night, although it seemed that everyone had the same idea, and I sat shoulder to shoulder with two other men doing our business. Not my finest hour.

Meanwhile back in the mozzipod, Buster was awake and looking grumpy as his warm human mattress had selfishly gone walkabout. 'Sorry Buster. Call of nature, my friend,' I explained as I folded myself back into my sleeping bag. Buster wasn't impressed and decided he wanted my pillow, even though it was not much bigger than a postage stamp. 'Buster, that's mine. You've got those furry ears to rest on; this, for what it's worth, is mine.' I made one final grab for the pillow before it disappeared under Buster's backside. After a couple of minutes the sleeping arrangements were sorted and Buster was curled up again on my feet. A couple of heavy dog sighs later and the usual trampling in circles routine, he and I must have finally drifted back off to sleep.

Boom!

The ground shook. I was awake and my heart was racing. I unzipped the mozzipod, reached out for my helmet, body armour and rifle.

Boom!

Another loud bang followed. I looked around and noticed that no one else was moving.

'Chan, Chan,' I called in a semi-shout-whisper.

'What?' came the reply.

'What was that?'

Chan didn't move but replied, 'They were ours, mate: 81 mm mortars going out.'

The 81 mm mortar can fire high explosive, illumination or infrared illumination rockets. Buster was wide awake and looking at me like I was his biggest disappointment. He gave me that 'you prat' look. Clearly Buster had known that they were Brit mortars, smart arse.

Eventually, I drifted off again but, what felt like only seconds later, there was another earth shattering explosion. My heart was coming through my ribcage and Buster was sitting on my chest. I gave him a reassuring hug.

'Will?' It was Chan.

'What mate?' I asked.

'Will, they are not ours this time,' he said.

'What do we do?'

Chan gave a second's thought and asked, 'Are you religious?'

I said, 'No, not particularly.'

Another second passed. 'Well sing a song or something then,' he said.

Then it dawned on me that I had a spaniel sitting on my chest and there was nowhere to take cover.

I gave Buster a shove, which landed him nowhere as he had glued himself to me, keeping us both on the ground. If it was dog instinct or indecision, I don't know, but it was the best place to be. Suddenly the black sky opened right up and the ground shook. It was the only sound to be heard. I lay there with Buster, shocked and deafened, not sure what was going to happen next. Buster didn't move and his calmness was good for me as it wasn't how I felt inside. I ruffled his ears and he shifted sideways, giving me the chance to roll onto my side. He took up position next to me and we lay with our heads down waiting for the next explosion. It didn't come.

'That's it folks,' said Chan. 'Just a little reminder they're watching us.'

He was right, it was the only explosion of the night, and in the morning we'd be able to survey the damage. The missile had landed just short of the compound, and a bit too close for comfort.

CHAPTER 5

Under Fire

I woke up at dawn. Some of the lads had already lit the fire to cook breakfast but as always my priority was Buster. He was as keen as I was to be out of the cramped mozzipod, and his nose followed my hand as I started to unzip. Buster dashed out as if he had been held prisoner in the thing. My chest was just about recovering from having been lain on, on and off throughout the night, and I didn't realise my legs were numb until I tried to get up. While I hopped about trying to bring some feeling back in my spaniel-trampled limbs, Buster set off to see who he could con into sharing their breakfast with him.

Clearly my request from the night before to hold back on feeding the greedy dog had been well and truly forgotten, because when I appeared all I could see was ration packs being offered up all over the place. Pathetically I limped after my begging dog in a vain attempt to remind people that over-feeding Buster was not only detrimental to his health but also to their safety. They reluctantly agreed and I made my way back to my hexi to boil my breakfast. Buster thought he'd just have to appeal to my better nature.

I used fresh bottled water to clean my teeth and put the rest into my cooking pot. After my breakfast ration pack had boiled to perfection I used some of the water to make a coffee and the rest to shave. Shaving is excused in the compound, but I have never liked having whiskers and had to shave at least every three days. My next job was to put in my contact lenses. I've never really liked messing with my eyes and in this environment, with the sand already ingrained in my fingers, it was now a painful chore. For several minutes my eyes streamed until the dirt had worked its way out. I noticed Buster return while I was testing my pain threshold and I'm sure he was laughing at me jumping around like an idiot. He had a look on his face that I was already very used to, the one that says, 'Get a grip man; it's just a bit of sand!' He sat with me for a while but I was obviously taking too long to get breakfast out so he went back to see if he had forgotten anyone else.

We were finishing up and gathering our kit when Lieutenant Bowers (sadly killed in Afghanistan in 2012) appeared to deliver a quick set of orders. We were to go out and reassure the locals that we were there for their security and, at the same time, gather information on Taliban presence in the area. It was also an opportunity to ask the local people face-to-face what they wanted from our protection and what would make life better for them. This isn't the part of the job that the folk back home immediately think of when they imagine us going about our duties.

Because Tracy is also in the RAF, I'm lucky that I have that understanding back home. I found it the most rewarding part of being in Afghan – the feeling that we are there to make a positive difference. The frustration was that it was such a battle. For me and Buster, I expected it to be a cultural battle too.

After the brief we set about sorting our kit. Again, enough supplies to last for twenty-four hours. Water, and plenty of it, was essential for both of us and the added carriage for me was Buster's food. We donned our protective gear, which meant full body armour, and made our way to the gate. I put Buster's harness on so he would know that he was on duty even before we left the compound. All eyes turned to the guys in the watchtowers, who would confirm the all-clear to proceed, and at the same time we made our weapons ready. I could sense every nerve in my body come alive making my skin tingle, but if Buster felt the same he didn't show it.

'You OK boy?' I said it all the same, although I knew he would look at me and say, 'Of course I am mate. How's about getting on with the job instead of acting like a jelly?' He was right, I was feeling a bit wobbly, but strangely that all left me as I saw Buster trotting off in front of the patrol.

There's something very reassuring about seeing him move so confidently in his work. I didn't want to let him down by dithering about, as he was relying on me to work ahead of him mentally by assessing the terrain. First he tested the air and then, once calibrated, set about trying to find his 'toys', shifting smoothly over the yellow dust, tail wagging and eager to find something to show me. Buster is naturally attracted to any prominent features such as lumps and bumps and piles of earth, and his training and instinct will lead him to check them out. As he searched a particular place, I looked for the next area that I wanted him to search. As we searched, the rest of the patrol provided security for us which meant that any locals who approached were stopped at a distance and asked to show what they were carrying. When we confirmed they weren't a danger to us or anyone else in the area, they were then allowed to proceed.

It didn't take long to clear the village and we soon found ourselves in the poppy fields. We walked through the black stalks, with the heat of the day pressing down as if it wanted to squash us into the sand – and the sun had still more to offer as it was nowhere near its peak. Buster was in full search mode, seemingly oblivious to the heat. The thing is, I knew he would search to the point of exhaustion and once this happened he was no longer any use. It was my job to make sure he was stopped before he got anywhere near that stage, otherwise the entire patrol was immediately in danger.

We stopped and the lads took up defensive positions all around while Buster took a break and had a well-earned drink. I think this was another reason the lads loved Buster so much – he gave them an excuse to stop more often and hopefully get some respite from the heat. It was hot and most of us were ready to drop, I know I was, and just a few minutes' rest was good enough to find an extra boost to keep moving. But it's not safe to stay in one place too long, you never know who's watching and waiting for an easy target. Buster had taken on a load of water, had his neck cooled with more and been able to rest his little legs for long enough, so we set off again with him leading the way.

We came up on several farmers and, through the interpreter, Locky chatted to them – asking how they were getting on and if there was anything they needed. Several were given dollar bills to help them out and hopefully put them on our side. I noticed how they all wore a troubled look – most likely a reflection of the reality that war was a constant part of their lives and had been for a long time.

To my surprise, the farmers honed in on Buster. It turned out, once again, that Buster was the star of the show. He didn't mind, even if they didn't have food to offer him (and he did check this out with a quick sniff), they were keen to fuss over him and he never refused a good fuss. He sat at my feet and each time one of them approached he looked to me, I'm guessing to get approval – after all we were still in uniform and so still at work. Several of the men offered money for him but when I told them he was worth $90,000 they quickly gave up on the idea of taking Buster off my hands! That's more than any Afghani would earn in ten lifetimes. I don't think that the average farmer knew what Buster was there for and we certainly weren't going to tell them. I can imagine that they would have gladly paid out if they knew what he is capable of. A great many Afghanis had already fallen victim to IEDs and legacy mines, they could have put him to great use.

It was good to see the local people warm to Buster in that way: warm to any dog in that way. It was not the reaction I had expected and seeing Buster walk so closely with us probably wasn't what they expected either.

It was time to move the patrol down to the bank of the Helmand River, where Buster took the opportunity to jump in for a cooling dip. All we could do was look on as we wilted in the heat. All seemed to be going well and Buster was doing his job, so we agreed it was time to stop for something to eat – Buster's other favourite pastime. Out came the ration packs, this time the cold snack variety, and it was only a matter of seconds before Buster got whiff of the first pouch being opened and left the river at his heels.

Good job we had been so jealous of Buster's river dipping, because he decided to bring some of the river to us. Dashing into the middle of the group he shook his whole, wet body. 'Aw Buster, that's just what we needed mate, a shower while we're sitting in a dust bowl!' The tiny splashes that Buster flung from his coat and onto our faces were actually really welcome, even though they evaporated the instant they landed on our skin.

Buster was working well and I allowed him the chance to lick out a tuna packet or two. He was going to need the extra energy to keep up the pace. We stayed in the shade of the trees for a while, avoiding the midday heat. The rest of the lads were pretty much acclimatised but it was still unbearably hot even for them. The sweat was running into my eyes and oozing from every pore. It was a great relief to take off my helmet for a while and enjoy the small pool of shade that was almost filled by Buster. He was multi-tasking: lying in the shade and being alert to the sound of rustling food wrappers.

Brief respite over, the patrol re-formed and left the shade for the open fields. It was not much after midday and the fields were empty as no one works when the sun is at its full height. Walking over the newly ploughed and scorched earth was hard going and, according to the naked eye, there wasn't much there to search, so Buster just tagged along with the patrol.

Crack!

'Incoming!' Locky shouted out, as rounds whizzed past us. The crack and spit of AK-type weapons was suddenly deafening and I looked for Buster who I could see just ahead. As I called him, he turned to face me and scampered over as the bullets whizzed past us and tore through the poppy stalks. Tiny puffs of sand jumped up from the ground as the rifle shots danced around us. And for the first time in my career I now understood the full meaning of the term 'effective enemy fire'.

My heart was racing and the adrenaline kicked in right away. The whole patrol was down in an instant and looking for the enemy, but Buster was playing it cool, not at all bothered about all the fuss. 'For Heaven's sake Buster get your arse down,' but the more I tried to wrestle him lower to the ground, the more he resisted. 'Do you want a bullet in your head or what you daft dog?' As I battled with a stiff-bodied spaniel the exchange of fire was happening all around us. I quickly secured Buster to my webbing with his lead and for the first time in twenty-three years fired my weapon in anger. The initial dread quickly turned to that weird excitement again. Our rifle fire was deafening as several weapons joined in the firefight. A heavy metallic smell of cordite hung in the air and attacked my nostrils.

The exchange ended as suddenly as it had begun. The lads explained that it was a typical Taliban 'shoot and scoot' tactic: if they didn't immediately hit a soldier, they quickly retreated, always out-gunned and tactically inferior. I looked to Buster, who had eventually decided to lie down. Was it fear, boredom, or just his uncanny ability to take it all in his stride? I don't know, but he certainly didn't look as stressed as the rest of us.

We regrouped and made sure that there were no injuries. Rounds were counted and, as it had been relatively brief, there was no need for some of us to replenish others' supplies. We all put fresh magazines on. Even if you've only fired a couple of rounds, you want a full magazine on at all times. Nothing worse than getting into another firefight and finding that you've only got a couple of rounds left. I gave Buster a big hug before I checked over his harness and made a good search of his body, to make sure he hadn't taken a hit and was just being a brave old sod about it. He was totally unfazed by the experience and eager to return to the search but I'm glad I took him to one side before we moved on. I wanted to make sure he was feeling OK, especially as he still had to do the most important job of keeping us safe.

The insurgents were now aware of our position. They also knew we had the advantage of a bomb dog on the team, but that wouldn't deter them from planting IEDs along our return route. It was now up to Buster to keep his cool for one last stretch of the patrol. Almost machine-like, he shrugged off the Taliban attack and got on with his job. I couldn't help but admire that and hope that he hadn't felt my hands shake as I adjusted his harness.

Once again all eyes and faith rested on Buster as he made safe our path back to the compound. We immediately shed our helmets and sweat-soaked clothes. A few lads dropped into their mozzipods and some grabbed a food pouch and headed for the fire pit. I could tell that Buster was close to exhaustion and, like everyone else, in need of water, food and rest.

I knelt down to Buster and stripped his harness off

his back, and offered him some water straight from the bottle. As we sat together, I stroked his silky head and fluffed-up his coat, which was thick with dust from the road. There was a little spring missing from his step and I guessed he needed to sit down as much as the rest of us. I saw Chan sitting by the fire pit so, with Buster almost attached to my legs, I walked over. As soon as my bottom hit the ground Buster moved in and slumped at my side. With a loud sigh and one big stretch of his tired body he lay with his back touching the full-length of my thigh and planted his head in the dirt. He was asleep. And while he slept I spoke to Chan about the contact.

He was very good and listened to me relive the events of the day, but I could see that what was a big encounter for me was, for him just another patrol in the horrible place that is the Green Zone. As we chatted we half-watched Buster who was having one of his 'action dreams', yelping, twitching and lips curling over his teeth. I hoped that he was chasing pheasants in the green grass of home rather than insurgents in the Afghan desert. It was funny to watch and he attracted a bit of a crowd.

I'm not sure if it was the lads laughing that woke him up or he managed to catch that pheasant, but he suddenly opened one eye. Right away he fixed on my dinner pouch, jumped up, shook himself off and took up position right under my nose. He must have been reminded that he was hungry so I put his well-earned tea into the pot and after we had both finished eating we listened to our orders for the next day. For Buster and me, it was checkpoint duty.

It was getting dark, so I climbed into my mozzipod and Buster followed. He looked disappointed as if he had been promised a room of his own only to discover that he was expected to bunk in with me – again. He uttered his second sigh of the evening before shuffling in and curling up on my feet. As I lay there, I was thinking about the day's events and how I had probably gone through every emotion known to man: fear to elation and everything in between. I was also thinking how it could have turned out so differently.

'Buster, come up here mate,' I said, guiding him onto my chest. 'What a day we've had and I'm sorry to say there will be a few more just like it. I want to tell you I was proud of you today, especially as you did a lot less shaking than I did my friend. I'm glad you were there and I know the others were glad too. You soft git.'

I gave him a big fuss before breaking the news, 'It's checkpoint duty for us tomorrow and you know how you love searching vehicles? Well, there's going to be a lot of them, maybe not as many as there were at Bastion, but there's one thing in its favour – there's likely to be a lot less gunfire than today. Well, I hope so. Night, then.'

In the middle of our chat Buster landed me with a big wet kiss. Yes, I was missing home and Tracy, but when he settled himself on my chest, I curled my arms around him. I needed to talk about the bad day at work, and this time Buster was the one listening. He was a massive comfort to me. I know I was luckier than most, just because I had him to talk to.

CHAPTER 6

River Dog

The checkpoint consisted of a rectangle of Hesco measuring about 40 by 20 metres, with a sentry post at one end where local farmers were stopped and searched both going in and out of the fields. We'd walked to our new posting in the relative 'cool' of the early morning. It was proving a slow day with only a handful of locals passed through and, although they weren't exactly friendly, they weren't threatening or hostile either. We were lucky that we had missed the height of the poppy harvest, as the constant traffic of vehicles – cars, vans, camels and donkeys all laden with the crop – would have been full-on. We were down to a straggle of random lorries, cars and motorcycles in our search for the 'other' harvest that goes on all year – the crop of IEDs, weapons and ammunition.

At the other end of the checkpoint was a bridge crossing the river to the fields and another sentry post. Buster had the company of thirteen lads to distract him from the boredom of repetitive vehicle checks and I had to keep him on top of his game by hiding practise items so he could have the 'buzz' of making a 'find' and the praise that goes with it. We both needed to stay sharp.

I'd been told I would be here for a couple of days, so the next patrol out would bring my extra supplies. They passed through a few hours later with kit for myself, a couple of other lads and the interpreter. As I looked through my stuff I realised that some of the most important bits were missing, including my head torch, Leatherman multi-tool and iPod. I wasn't best pleased. I don't know if Buster sensed my disappointment or my fit of expletives got him going but a little while later he decided to conduct his own search and paid the interpreter a visit. When I followed up, the guy was sitting there with all the stuff in front of him as if it was his birthday, obviously they had been mixed up in the move. Buster decided to guard it all until I had sorted it out, but I still felt a bit of a spoilsport reclaiming it all – the guy was visibly disappointed. I wondered whether to claim this as Buster's first big find of the tour! Certainly the most important as far as I was concerned.

Once nightfall came we relaxed with the lads, hearing more stories of their tour, some hilarious, some horrific, and I'll admit that I went to sleep that night with tales of daring and sadness going through my head. Those young lads had all been through the loss of their colleagues. They had survived what was to become a famous assault on the Taliban base Jugroom Fort in Garmsir. The lads didn't know the full story at that point, but it later became known that four Royal Marines strapped themselves to Apache helicopters to retrieve the body of one of their fallen comrades.

Our lads had their own terrors to cope with. They saw young men cut down in their prime, but those young men probably wouldn't have wanted to go any other way. Heroes one and all. Mac told me that the fort was a wonder to behold with its labyrinth of underground tunnels used as escape routes by the Taliban, and I built a mental picture of rats running through sewers.

Yet again Buster had been the perfect listener and a real hit with his new friends, who gave him plenty of attention.

The day had been pretty relaxed and now with my toys back in my hands I was happy enough to turn in for the night. We were still sleeping in one-man mozzipods on our roll mats, so I was ready to do the nightly 'who's sleeping where' tango with Buster before being allowed to get some kip. I had taken a look at the toilet arrangements earlier and it got me thinking that I really didn't want to make any trips to the loo overnight – this time our toilet was a six foot hole with an anti-tank rocket rail to sit on for solids, which looked like a hazardous place to set foot in the dark. Once settled in the mozzipod Buster bustled around the place swirling and sniffing but at least he waited until I had my whole body inside before making a rush for the pillow. He must have thought it was worth making a bid for the comfy bit, until I reminded him that I was in charge. I shifted him down to my feet and after about ten minutes we compromised with him settling on my legs. To be honest I was too tired to put up a convincing fight.

I awoke at around 0530 with Buster sat bolt upright on my feet. As I struggled to gain focus Buster didn't move a muscle. He sat solid as a rock. Bleary eyed I followed the line of his snout to find out what he was staring at. His eyes were bulging and his front paws started to pad about on my shins and as I sat up I could see why. A group of four locals were leading a train of camels through the checkpoint on the bridge. 'Camels, Buster. Nothing to worry about. You ignore them and they will ignore you. Let's have a bit more kip and then some breakfast.' I could see that Buster was adding 'camels' to his mental list of sights and smells of the desert.

I think he would have preferred to investigate for himself rather than taken my word for it, as the whole padding and circling, shifting and shuffling thing started all over again. Breakfast came earlier than planned so Buster could escape the mozzipod to check if the camels had gone and I could escape being trodden on in my tender spots. He waited patiently for his share of a boil-in-the-bag all-day breakfast and then helped himself to a leftover packet of tuna offered by another hungry insomniac. If I had been more awake I would have vetoed the tuna, only because I knew we would both suffer the after-effects of such an explosive food combination in the mozzipod that evening.

We allowed ourselves a slow start that morning, but by the time we were heading for the checkpoint on the bridge is was already 32 degrees and rising. Buster was in his working harness so his stride was purposeful, but he was panting like a paunchy jogger. 'Slow down boy, you can't move that fast in this bloody heat or you'll keel over you daft dog.' That helpful advice came from me, weighed down in full body armour and doing my best to keep up without being the first one of us to collapse.

I was ambling at pace but still couldn't help marvel at the never-ending expanse of ochre-coloured earth that spread way off into the distance, meeting the horizon at a striking purple line. To the right of us, a hill marked the path travelled by the locals approaching from Gereshk. Dirt tracks from all directions converged at this place, creating something resembling a kind of rough roadway leading to the checkpoint. Serving in Northern Ireland and Bosnia had taught me to instinctively scan and assess any terrain before venturing too boldly into it. As I clocked the hills and traffic coming towards the checkpoint I knew this road from Gereshk was the most likely direction from which an attack would be launched.

Tractors and motorbikes joined the stream of farm vehicles moving forward for inspection, our day's work was building up already. I think Buster clocked it all too. As soon as he saw all the vehicles forming an orderly line he stopped and sat down. 'What's up, mate? Don't fancy searching today?' I said it knowing that if he could speak Buster would tell me what I could do with my vehicle search. He didn't budge.

'Come on. I know you can think of something better to do but this is the best I can offer today, my friend, so let's go and get on with it.' I signalled ahead and I think he got the message that there was no way out of it. He wasn't happy.

There was procedure that had to be followed: as the vehicles reached the 40 metre point, the cover guards yelled 'Stop!', which brought everything to a standstill. This morning the procedure didn't go immediately to plan, and a mini-flare was sent into the air above the uncooperative drivers. 'Get off the vehicle,' the interpreter stepped in to repeat the request.

Once everyone had done as they were asked the searcher stepped forward of the sentry post and, in what I can only describe as air stewardess-like fashion, used exaggerated hand signals to issue the next request: first raise their hands to show they are empty, then lift their 'dish-dash' (*dishdasha*, traditional male robe) and turn to prove they are not carrying a weapon or wearing a suicide vest. Next they remove their headdress. (The turbans worn by the Afghanis are not religious headwear and so it is not disrespectful to ask them to remove them – the Taliban used this myth for a long time to smuggle things past troops.) This time the searcher was happy and so moved forward with the interpreter to start the questioning. Meanwhile, Buster went about his business searching the vehicles and the trailers.

If you've never seen an Arms and Explosives Search dog go about their work it's difficult to imagine how intent and purposeful they can be. I've had good dogs in my time but from the first day I worked with Buster

I could tell that he was special. He has a style all of his own. First he checks in with me – just a second of eye contact – then his nose is up. Nothing can distract him from his job. His nose runs like a vacuum cleaner hose over the search area and he won't leave what he is doing until he has completed his task. All the time his stumpy tail is wagging, which makes his liver-and-white body blur a little as he moves along. And this is where Buster is king. To do the same thorough job a team of soldiers would have to unload, sift and then reload the cargo on each vehicle, a process that takes hours.

We soon got used to seeing vehicles going in empty and then returning packed with vegetables or dried poppy stems, and Buster kept both the locals and soldiers happy with his quick and efficient turnover. By midday, the temperature was well into the 40s and we were sweating like crazy. As with everything in Afghan, when the sun reaches its highest point, everything and everyone stops.

Zac, the section 2 lance corporal, told us that if we wanted we could go for a swim in the river. In an instant of hearing the words 'swim' and 'river' Buster whirled round in the direction of the water. From a tired and restless dog, Buster was now a spaniel on a mission.

Long ears flowing, tongue lolling and feathery feet kicking up dust, Buster was halfway to the river bank before I could grab my washing, soap and a bucket. He launched himself into the water with a mighty splash and while I was still wrestling out of my T-shirt, Buster was belly deep in the cool, shallow water.

Celebrating his watery 'find', Buster looked at me as if to say: 'Look at me aren't I clever?' But no sooner had he thrown me his wide-eyed 'come on in and play' look than his expression changed to sheer panic. As he had paddled away from the slow side-stream of the river, the current suddenly swept Buster into the middle and in no time at all he was heading off in the direction of the Kajaki Dam!

'Buster! Buster! You knob end, get back here!' I shouted. Others shouted his name over and over to grab his attention but he was just drifting further downstream.

By now my head had already moved into Emergency Plan A overdrive. How could I get ahead of my rapidly drifting dog and then magically pull him from the water? In the minutes it took me to panic and imagine the sight of Buster washed-up dead downstream, he had clearly worked something out. Based entirely on dog logic, which I've learned is far more reliable than the human version, Buster had devised an escape plan.

The troubled glare and furrowed brow disappeared. He suddenly realised that the river was only going to carry him so far. As the current changed, the pull of the water left him able to swim back up to his friends. I'm sure he was smiling so much I could see his teeth – he didn't need me to panic after all. This was now his new game: going with the flow and then swimming back!

While Buster had fun, I took turns with the other guys as we washed ourselves and our clothes in the cool water. Some of the lads in the section kept watch, weapons ready for any sudden attacks, while the rest of us carried out our laundry chores. We did this in ten minute shifts: ten minutes in and then ten minutes out of the water, so everyone had a chance to enjoy the moment. But when I say everyone got out after ten minutes, I mean everyone except Buster. When you see a spaniel in water it's sometimes hard to see where the dog ends and the water begins. Buster is a pretty sturdy individual, and sometimes he can be a bit 'ploddy' on dry land, but in the water his silky lines blur into its liquid folds. It's a bit like watching an otter gliding and swirling underwater: one minute you see their body glistening above the surface and the next they are part of the water.

Buster's idea of fun didn't have anything to do with waiting on the river bank, for him it was all about diving in and 'helping' everyone else to do their washing! To see big, rough, tough soldiers wading in the river to wash their clothes and then Buster dashing in and romping off with their rolled-up socks (they look roughly like a ball) was hilarious. Even the guys who had to give chase and wrestle their socks from his jaws saw the funny side. We could have been enjoying this bit of water sport anywhere in the world but the reality check was we were in Afghan and being guarded by colleagues in full body armour, carrying rifles who had their eyes on the hills beyond.

After just five minutes out of the water our clothes were completely dry and sweating up again. We had been on this spot for some time and there was a restlessness now and a sense that it was time to move on, but first I had to get Buster out of the river.

'Good luck with that Sergeant,' shouted Zac. 'We'll see you for breakfast!'

To roars of laughter I called Buster out, 'OK Buster that's enough. Out you come now. Buster! Buster!'

Although generally obedient this time he decided to adopted selective hearing and turned his back on me. I didn't blame him for wanting extra time in the river, after all, none of us were in a rush to get back out into the baking sun.

The more I shouted the quicker he moved towards the middle of the river. He knew that in full kit plus body armour, I was pretty unlikely to wade in after him. A relatively lightweight springer spaniel paddling in the river is one thing, but to have a fourteen stone airman laden with seventy to eighty pounds of equipment, food and ammunition sinking before everyone's eyes is another.

'For crying out loud Buster, get here now!'

He could tell he had pushed me to the limit but being in water meant so much to him and this time he wasn't going to give in without a bit of a fight. There was no way I was going in there after him and I think he eventually got that message. He gave himself a massive shake-off and sprinted over to me. He sat bolt upright at my feet and looked dead ahead – the springer spaniel version of standing to attention. I couldn't help reaching down and giving the old dog a good fuss.

Sometimes he's not a dog at all he's like a mate, one of the lads. When he messes about and shows a side of his character you wish he could talk so we could have some really good boy banter. I sometimes think he is really a person trapped in a fur coat. He looks at you as if he understands every word you say and in an odd way he gives you answers. I can't explain it I just know that's who Buster is.

But then, as every dog handler will tell you, we're glad that dogs understand us but can't speak. That's for one reason only – they know all of our deepest secrets.

Buster looked very pleased with himself after his first real playtime in the water, and from now on took every opportunity to make his way to the river, his new favourite place.

But like most things in Afghan, all was not as it appears. Shallow at the edge, it took just a few unmeasured steps before you were in waist deep. Dirty brown from a distance but clear close-up, I would guess the river was about 20 metres wide, but goodness knows how deep.

On each side there was lush vegetation and trees, and an aroma of wet earth and sweet foliage. One thing was for sure, the river was the lifeblood of the area – the only thing keeping anything alive in a hostile environment where all you can taste, smell and breathe is sand.

But add a dog to the scene and suddenly it doesn't matter that there are guns and men in uniform, because dogs are a universal joy. For the men that day, Buster provided a momentary and much appreciated reminder of home and normality in a very dangerous and uncertain place.

The next day started much the same as the previous one, quickly falling into the routine of having breakfast, washing and getting to work. The early morning was always pleasant: the cool of the night gradually giving way to the warmth of the day, but we all knew that in a just a few hours the sun would be punishing.

As always, my first priority was Buster and getting him exercised, fed and watered and ready for a day's work, which, to his huge disappointment, was another day of searching farm vehicles and random cars and the odd cart passing through the checkpoint. But as I was rinsing my mess-tin-come-shaving-bowl-come-basin the earth shook. The ground was literally moving under my feet. I looked to Buster to see if he had felt it but he was otherwise engaged with a biscuit.

The ground shaking turned to rumbling, which went on for some time until it all came to a stop with that distinctive screech of metal on metal. The Vikings had mounted the bridge and what an imposing sight they made. They were delivering supplies, including water and rat packs, so a chain was quickly formed to unload everything and get it safely away. While we worked on the line, Buster stood with the bearing of a WWII sergeant major, supervising the operation and no doubt visualising the treasures inside the boxes. The marines made a beeline for Buster, giving him lots of fuss, but if he was looking for the guy who offered him the pig's ear the first time we encountered the Vikings he was going to be disappointed. This time he had to make do with an overdose of special and full-on fuss.

Suddenly a loud man-scream came from behind the pile of supplies. I looked over to see people jumping off the top of the Vikings, boxes being dropped all over the place and guys running all over the shop. I reached for my weapon, with some of the other lads, and moved towards the chaos. Before we got close enough to see what was going on the screaming turned to laughter and a round of choice expletives. The source of the alarm – a two-inch scorpion that had hitched a ride on the rat pack boxes. The problem with scorpions is the smaller they are, the deadlier they can be, and this one was capable of delivering a sting that would probably put a grown man in need of a casevac (casualty evacuation) and could have killed Buster. But still, all the serious stuff aside, it was very comical to see these battle-hardened soldiers running around like little girls because of a creepy-crawly. It would take a while to shake that one off.

Thankfully Buster kept his distance. For once he didn't think he was missing anything and barge in as he normally would if he saw an audience. He had found himself a shady spot beneath one of the piles of boxes, which, thinking in Buster terms, was THE prime spot if anyone happened to open one of them and put a rat pack on to boil!

Job done, the Vikings set off into the desert looking menacing with their vast array of weaponry spiking the space around them. Crewed by some of the world's toughest soldiers, just the sight of them rumbling through the desert must have sent waves of fear through the ranks of the Taliban. I was always glad they were on our side.

We then settled back into our duties. A tractor with five local people on board chugged up to the checkpoint and, as per routine, the driver was ordered to stop the vehicle and everyone to get down. A young soldier approached with the interpreter while I waited in cover with Buster. The soldier put his hands up and the locals copied him, they had clearly been through the process before and that always made it easier for everyone. The soldier then pulled his hand down to his shoulders, then over to one side and the locals did the same. It took a couple of seconds before I realised what was happening – he had these village people doing the 'YMCA' dance!

I know that might sound unprofessional or demeaning but within minutes the soldiers and the villagers were laughing together. I doubt the locals had ever heard of the 'YMCA' song, but the ice was broken and from that day these particular individuals always had a laugh and a joke with our lads. Neither side understood exactly what the other was saying but somehow there was an understanding between them that made a difference. It was a relationship that proved useful too because they started to give us good intelligence on Taliban whereabouts and movements in the area.

The next day the earth moved again as the Vikings reappeared and made their presence felt. This time they weren't delivering supplies – they had come to collect Buster. He had been selected for special desert patrol duties so I was ordered to gather our kit immediately for the off. We were moving out right away to conduct a series of snap vehicle checkpoints (VCPs). This is where we stop, get out, check a couple of vehicles, mount up and go somewhere else, never staying long at any one location, as it would give the insurgents too much time to mount an attack.

Buster had a particular liking for the Vikings, probably because the marines were always so generous with their treats and fuss. The noisy arrival of the vehicles sent shivers down most mortals' spines but Buster associated it with the promise of massive attention. Having the advantage of super-sensitive canine hearing, he could hear them coming long before the rest of us, which explained why he had been giving it plenty of tail wagging and padding about before they came into human view. Buster was excited and when he saw me gathering our stuff he must have guessed were taking a day off vehicle searches at the checkpoint.

When you don't have much in the way of kit it's relatively easy to pack the essential food and water for man and dog. In no time at all we were in the belly of the Viking in the stifling heat and dreaming of a cooling dip in the river. But Buster was always a good traveller – as long as he could sit on a seat that is – and this time he didn't have to use his charm or shift his weight around to get a place next to me. The lads were happy to accommodate the bold and cheeky bomb dog so I didn't have to play the bad cop.

It seemed odd to suddenly stop in the middle of nowhere where there was nothing but sand for miles and miles. But it turned out that the discoloured strip beneath our feet was actually a road which the Vikings used as a guideline for pushing out to create a defensive perimeter, ready to intercept anyone who tried to avoid inspection. From this point we watched and waited. There was a long and hot pause before we saw a huge cloud of sand moving on the horizon. The patrol prepared for the first spot check of the day.

The vehicle approached and the driver was ordered to stop and then everyone was ordered out of the vehicle. It was a small car, probably a Toyota Corolla, a favourite car in those parts, and I watched in amazement as four men climbed out of the front and four more unfolded themselves from the back seat. After each one had been searched, Buster was sent to work on the car to make sure there were no hidden surprises for the lads, who followed up with a search for intelligence. Maps, photographs and handwritten notes on scraps of paper often provided clues to Taliban activity, but on this occasion the car was clean. We watched in amazement as all eight men squeezed back in and drove off waving and smiling. I hoped they didn't have far to go as they looked very hot and uncomfortable!

Within moments we were all loaded back into the Viking and heading for our second location which was close to the river, where a few small trees and low bushes added colour to the orange landscape. What caught my interest was a small shelter constructed from branches, which looked like the perfect hiding place for an IED. I asked three of the lads to cover me as I worked Buster along the path towards it. He stopped and wagged his tail. If he was telling me there was nothing dangerous in there I was happy to believe him and approached it to look inside. Right away I came face-to-face with a very startled family of four, who clearly weren't expecting visitors.

As I looked around I realised that this was their home. All they had was two chairs, a small table, and some straw matting and blankets. The branches were a covering for the basic wooden hut, which was about the size of something we would use to store our garden tools in back home. I had Buster close by me and he couldn't resist poking his head through the doorway, which must have scared the poor folks to death. Suddenly there were four armed soldiers and a bustling sniffer dog in their living room. They were probably too shocked to do anything about it so Buster took advantage of the situation by making a beeline for the children who were soon laughing and fussing over the furry intruder.

In Northern Ireland and Bosnia, I'd found a dog could be a great asset: if the people were unsure about you, there was a huge chance the dog would dissolve the barriers. To my surprise, it was proving effective nine times out of ten in Afghanistan too. When we left the family everyone was smiling and waving – mostly at Buster, who had been rolling out all his party tricks and grabbing everyone's attention. I knew I would have to issue a pretty firm order to get him to leave. The children huddled up next to him and, I'm guessing, said goodbye to him, which Buster rewarded with a second look back as they waved from the door of their tiny home.

As we walked back to our vehicle a small van approached. The usual routine was carried out with the driver and passengers ordered out of the vehicle. The driver was very agitated as he was being searched, although nothing was found on him or his friends.

But his muttering and jumpiness got a whole lot worse when he saw Buster weaving around the outside of the van and then jump inside.

Immediately Buster went from laid-back to overdrive. He put his nose in the air and his tail started to wag.

He was onto something.

'Get back lads,' I alerted everyone just in case, as he was all over the van and not missing an inch of any part of it.

Suddenly he jumped over the back seat and stopped by the wheel cover, where he performed his special little growl and dance – he had found something.

Now we had a problem – was it a bomb or a weapon?

I called Buster to me while the driver and interpreter spoke to the patrol commander, who wanted more specific information before sending a man in. When the driver was questioned he insisted that it was a hunting rifle. I felt a chill run down my spine.

The guy slowly lifted the cover to reveal two AK-47s. I don't know what they hunt in Afghanistan, but this seemed a bit excessive for a rabbit – which is probably why the occupants of the van were promptly photographed, handcuffed and escorted to Camp Bastion in one of the Vikings.

'Well done Buster!' I was so proud of him, but it wasn't just me congratulating the old lad on his 'find'. The other guys were crowded around giving him plenty of praise too. The boy had done good! To have a 'find' with a dog is always a great feeling, but when you know you may have just saved lives it's even better. He got his play with the tennis ball, and he was going to get a few extra treats that night for sure – and that was just from me.

The celebrations had to be cut short, though, as we still had a couple more VCPs to conduct before we were dropped back at the checkpoint. News of the 'find' had reached there ahead of us, guaranteeing Buster a hero's welcome. I'm sure his chest puffed out and his tail wagged just a little bit faster. Everyone wanted to say their own personal 'well done' to him, which, in turn, made me feel a big part of the MERCIAN regiment from that day on.

CHAPTER 7

Pulling the Pin

Not every day in Afghan is filled with a sense of foreboding, it's just most of the days and nights that are played out in the shadow of terror and uncertainty, and that's what Buster and I experienced on checkpoint duty. Manning the checkpoint was our daily routine for quite some time, but there was no room for complacency. There was always a nagging thought that the next vehicle to pull up could be the one carrying the bomb with your name on it. The next patrol you're on could be the one where a sniper cuts your day and your life short. I always had to watch Buster swagger into danger first, and I hated it because he always treated his work out there as a game – locate the 'find' and he gets to play with his favourite tennis ball – but I knew that it was a deadly game and Buster was a prime target for the enemy and a far greater prize than me.

The highlight of any day out there for Buster was a cooling dip in the river – and mealtimes. After about twenty-five days on rat packs you start to imagine all kinds of home-cooked food so when a local man checked through with his load of potatoes and several loaves of bread there was only one thing on our minds. We collected a dollar from everyone and bought all he was carrying, which pleased him no end as our dollars added up to the equivalent of six months' wages in one go. We lit a fire and poured cooking oil into an ammunition tin, which that day doubled as a deep fat fryer. Within fifteen minutes we had found some sachets of salt and vinegar (amazing what soldiers carry in their kit) and had a chip butty in hand. Absolute heaven!

Unless you've ever done boil-in-a-bag for any length of time, you could never appreciate the sheer delight of that butty. It was such a treat that even Buster did not get much of a look in, much to his disgust. He wasn't impressed with reduced hand outs but he had more than enough for a working dog, and thankfully it was enough to help him sleep well that night.

That was our last supper with our pals at the checkpoint. The next day we were collected and returned to The Fan where Buster was welcomed as the hero of the hour and picked up where he had left off with his old friends. We had only been away a short time but there had been a special delivery of cot beds which Buster spotted immediately. The sight of a comfy bed sent him into a mad moment running around and checking out the new furniture by trampling all over them until he found one to linger on. Buster remembered his friend Chan and invited himself to the dog-loving soldier's cot to share a romantic tuna sachet moment.

It was good to be back 'home' with Chan and the other lads, but we knew there wouldn't be time to rest on our laurels. Buster was in demand and we needed to make the most of the Vikings before they disappeared on patrol again. We were driving along when the top cover gunner reported sighting disturbed earth on the track. That was our cue to get out and search ahead, so I harnessed Buster and we jumped out onto the raised track, which had a ditch to the left and the Helmand River on our right. The contrast between the barren, dry earth on the one side and the lush foliage on the other was incredible. It was also prime IED territory, and sure enough about 75 metres in front was an area of disturbed earth.

We usually try to use the wind to our advantage, but there was not even the slightest breeze for Buster to get his nose into, which meant he needed to be almost on top of the area he was searching – on top of any device lurking there. I needed my wits about me, I needed to be one step ahead if he gave even the slightest indication. My body armour tightened around me and I could feel the adrenaline kicking in with the rush of sweat oozing from every pore. The lads had pushed out to watch the area from their sites and Buster was waiting patiently at my heel for my command to go in.

It was just him and me now. My intention was to treat this as a route search. It's a method that was perfected in Northern Ireland where the dog is sent down one side, crossed over and then brought back down the other. In the UK this is made easier thanks to the hedgerows forming natural boundaries, but it's nowhere near the same out in the desert, except in rare spots like this. I sent Buster on and kept his first leg short. He didn't waver, just kept his nose down and bustled on. On the second leg he hit the disturbance. I'm sure my heart stopped because he stopped. For what seemed like ages he had a good sniff over the site – and then moved on. I trust Buster absolutely and at this point I knew there was no risk from an IED – he simply wouldn't have missed it. My heart quickened anyway when I passed over the spot but I knew I wasn't going to meet my maker that day.

I could hear the others muttering versions of 'well done Buster' as we completed the search. We were so close to the river I decided that I would let Buster search down the left hand side, then cross over and swim back down the right, for a well-deserved cool off! It wasn't just to give Buster a treat, it also meant that he would be able to search for a longer distance in the incredible heat. Also as he was denied a 'find' I hoped that the fun of taking the river route would make up for some of the disappointment.

By the time we reached The Fan we were happy to be alive and Buster was a happy dog who still had the smell of the river about him. The smell of wet dog is never good, and the whiff of quick dried river dog is particularly nasty, but out there no one seemed to notice and if they did they didn't care. We weren't exactly sweet smelling either. They hugged Buster and told him what a great and brave lad he was. Whiffy dog or not he was loving all the attention – and he deserved it.

It was another evening of celebration with Buster as the guest of honour. I told him he needed to 'get smartened up!' so he knew I would be after him for a good wash and brush up as soon as I had sorted the same for myself.

By now Buster was on speaking terms with just about everyone in the compound and was used to being able to come and go as he pleased, in and out of people's space and on and off their cots. So that evening after supper when he wandered off on his rounds I thought nothing of it until I heard Afghan voices raised and some weird clucking and flapping noises. I don't know why but I had a nagging suspicion that a certain spaniel could have something to do with it.

Dashing in the direction of the commotion, I reached the interpreters' room where all hell seemed to have been let loose – and guess who was in the middle of it all. Buster, it transpired, had burst past the blanket that was being used as a door and then mooched about a bit before introducing himself to one of the terp's prize chicken. As always, he only wanted to say 'hello' to the poor creature, but I think his intentions were lost in translation. The terp was shouting, 'My chicken! My chicken!' and trying to get a grip on the startled bird. Buster was sitting watching the show.

When I turned up I was lost for words, and it was lucky for all of us that he chose that moment to get bored and walk out. I'm not sure how I managed to explain everything away, maybe I didn't and the interpreters were just glad that no harm had been done. Either way there were no hard feelings the next day and Buster, the chicken and relationships were intact. Looking back, the reaction of the terp was hilarious.

The next day saw the Vikings depart in a crash of noise and diesel fumes. Buster sat and watched his friends leave the compound and then found a place where he could watch until they had disappeared into the block of haze on the horizon. He had a soft spot for the Vikings Troop.

That morning I'd allowed him to accept a few parting gifts, not for Buster's sake but for the men who had been saving bits for him from their breakfast or home parcel. I could see that Buster's dog power was needed 100 per cent. He had done his job well and gained the Royal Marines' respect. Unconditional love is not something you find lying around in the desert but Buster had heaps of it to give out.

Once they had left, The Fan felt very exposed. The Vikings' presence had been awesome and I'm sure played a part in keeping the Taliban at arm's length even for the few days they were with us. Anyone who served later will probably think I'm talking rubbish and that the Vikings are death traps. Since I was there, the IED threat grew, with each blast bigger than the last. After several lethal 'killings' of Vikings, the vehicles had to be called in to improve their armour. They are now called the Warthog. I probably wouldn't trust a Viking now, but at the time we were also driving round in Snatch Land Rovers and for very similar reasons I certainly wouldn't do that again either. The fact is they served their purpose at the time and I'm living proof that they served pretty well.

With the Vikings gone we also had to walk everywhere. It's a good thing that many of the patrols were hazard-free. After all, that's the situation we were aiming for and a sign that we were gaining the locals' trust in us and our purpose for being there. They would often come out and greet us, especially the children who would head straight for Buster – who was of course happy to lap up the perks of his developing celebrity status.

At one compound the village elder invited us all in for tea which, no matter how you take yours, is always very sweet and very hot. Of course, drinking the water and eating the food was a big issue for our digestive systems, but when you're there on a 'hearts and minds' operation it would be hugely impolite to refuse, so we tucked in.

Buster had to stay outside, so the lads took turns looking after him. When it came back round to my turn to check on him I thought the circus had come to town. He was surrounded by the villagers, young and old alike, talking to him, stroking him – all clearly mesmerised by my dog. I had to ask him, 'You OK

Buster? Would you like any more attention?' His soft brown eyes were all scrunched up with sheer pleasure. He was loving every minute of it and single-handedly destroyed the myth that Muslims don't like dogs.

Patrols were unpredictable. Some were meant to be little more than 'social calls' to engage with the local people, reassure them, and sometimes hand out money in the hope they would invest it in growing a less toxic crop than opium. We always left with high hopes. But the nature of the patrol was that it could always swing the other way and what had been a peaceful day visiting a string of compounds talking to ordinary hard-working people struggling with abject poverty became a stark reminder that this was a war zone and we were not on a Sunday School outing.

One morning's visits seemed particularly uneventful, one meeting blending into another. Buster was restless. He wasn't being a bother but he was in constant search mode and not finding anything. He enjoyed the meeting and greeting part of the job, but at the same time, he knew that he was there to work and maybe it didn't feel like work to him.

We were searching another poppy field, when suddenly Buster stood to attention and thrust his nose in the air. I knew he had heard something, but I couldn't see what it could be and put it down to dog-stuff.

Crack! Crack! Crack!

We were suddenly exposed to the all too familiar sound of gunfire. The treeline was about 40 metres away to our left and it was the only cover available for miles around. The others hit the ground while I dived into a drainage ditch, dragging Buster with me. We landed in a bit of a heap of arms and legs but I was more worried about the increasing exchange of shots.

The noise was deafening as we returned rapid fire, and all the time Buster was curled up by my feet. Seeing him so cool and collected was a good thing for me because I was neither.

'Throw smoke!' The order went out to release our red phosphorous grenades. I popped my head up, wanting to see the spectacle.

'Pop the bloody smoke!' More shouts echoed around and I looked to my right to see a few people staring at me. 'Will you pop the bloody smoke mate?'

To my horror I realised they were yelling at me to throw the thing as I had the best cover. I put my brain into rewind to recall the briefings on the grenades and remembered they have a blast radius of 30 metres – and I throw like a girl!

I took it out of the pouch and I'm sure that the lads thought I was reading the instructions or something, the amount of time I was taking. 'Throw the bloody thing – now!' I pulled the ring and pulled back my arm to launch the grenade. My heart was thumping, my mouth was dry and I was shaking and sweating in equal amounts. 'Thirty metres,' I kept saying it to myself, 'thirty metres.'

In that second, out of the corner of my eye, I saw Buster up on all fours looking very excited, tail wagging, and with total focus on my throwing arm. I knew exactly what he was thinking. Oh, no.

As I hurled the grenade with one hand, I stamped a foot back onto Buster's lead, just in time to bring him back to earth. My weight on the lead managed to stall him in full flight before he had a chance to chase down the grenade. He was going nowhere.

'For fuck's sake, Buster, are you trying to give me a heart attack or what?' I shouted, stepping back into the ditch. He looked puzzled, wondering why he couldn't chase the 'ball' that Dad had just thrown. 'You soft shit. Let's hope no one else noticed you did that.'

The grenade wasn't as loud as I thought it would be, but it was a spectacular sight, smothering the area with a thick blanket of red smoke. We all fired at the enemy and once again I felt euphoric at 'putting rounds down'. It's what we were there to do. The patrol ran past me and I followed with Buster glued to my heels. We all headed for the safety of the few trees and watched the crimson smog dilute to pink and then gradually fade to wisps of white.

Random bouts of small arms fire is bad on the nervous system but it makes you feel alive and alert. We looked to the line of trees knowing they couldn't provide dense cover but they were enough to protect us until the danger had passed and we could make our break back to the compound. Buster's expression was a mix of anger and disappointment – loping along, head hanging low with a weirdly furrowed brow – and I knew what he was trying to tell me in the best way he could. He had seen me with my arm raised over my head and he thought it was game on! And guess what? I went and spoilt it all.

By the time we got back to the compound we were all in need of a shower and drinking water – lots of it. We sorted the admin side of things and then the fatigue hit. The day's events had taken a dangerous turn and Buster, like the rest of us, was dusty and weary. Everyone gave him a bit of a fuss before we all dispersed to do our different things: some of the lads had food and some just collapsed on their beds.

I was pleased that no one mentioned his escapade with the smoke grenade. But later, over supper, I found out the reason why – they'd been saving it up and the laughs were on me. There were howls of laughter from the lads as they told their version of events and how I'd looked about to fill my trousers when I realised I had to throw the grenade and then stop Buster trying to retrieve it! I think the laughter was in part the relief that we had come through another piece of action miraculously unscathed. For these lads the end of tour was days away and must have been getting harder and harder.

Once again Buster did his rounds, visiting the lads and giving everyone a chance share a cuddle and a chat about their day. We now have a procedure called TRiM (Trauma Risk Management), which is used after traumatic incidents to see if our soldiers need further counselling. I think we should just train our dogs to do it, as I'm sure that our troops are a lot happier to admit their fears to them than they are to each other.

His round done, Buster came and jumped on my legs. I zipped up the mozzipod and lay down, listening to music and reading with my head torch on. Typical of Buster he had now made himself comfortable on my chest and was not for moving. He really didn't care how uncomfortable I was but then neither did I. I drifted off to sleep with the sound of 81 mm mortars being fired into the night. Amazing how quickly you get used to things.

A few nights later we were woken to the shouts of, 'Stand to, stand to,' coming from the watchtower. This meant that the enemy had been sighted or heard. Zips were quickly opened, body armour thrown on, weapons picked up and people dashed to predetermined positions.

All except me. The unzipping went well, Buster was heaved off and I jumped off my camp bed. That's when it went horribly wrong. Buster had had his full weight on my legs and now they just wouldn't work and I went down like a bag of the proverbial. As much as I tried, I couldn't get any life into them.

Eventually, my armour thrown on and weapon grabbed, I made my wobbly way to my place. Fortunately, it was a false alarm.

On the way back to our digs, a couple of the lads good-naturedly mimicked my stupid walk. I suppose I was asking for it, really – I must have looked ridiculous. Buster, in his usual way, looked like he was having a good laugh too.

Before I knew it, I had been there for over a month and our time with the MERCIANs was drawing to a close. The Coldstream Guards were coming to take over, which meant the MERCIANs could prepare for home. I made a phone call back to the Dog Unit and was told to leave with the lads and return to FOB Price. The incoming Guards were not happy. They were desperate to keep us there but sadly there are never enough dogs to go around. It was good to feel wanted and it would have been an honour to stay, but it was not meant to be.

On the last day, the Guards came in and the MERCIANs downloaded all their extra rounds and handed stores and ammunition over. I then got the section together and took a last photo of them with Buster. We all collapsed our shelters and packed our Bergans, which were all thrown onto the trailer to be transported to the helipad by the checkpoint.

It was to be our final patrol with the MERCIANs, a bunch of great lads who we had come to know very well in very short time. It had been a tough tour and they were going home without comrades who had fought and died alongside them. That would be harder to bear once the sand had worked its way out of their hair and clothes. We had been told the Chinooks were on their way out for us, so when we reached the checkpoint there was still time to sit and wait and also watch the Guards make the place their own. It's a strange thing in the military that no matter how well something works, when someone new comes in they feel that they have to make changes. The Royal Engineers had been hard at work, and the checkpoint was now much improved with extra Hesco all around it.

Sitting and surveying the scene we saw two local men sat in the grass by the river. A warning was shouted and a mini-flare fired in their direction and they headed off. They were probably just doing the same as us, taking five minutes, looking around, but you can't be too careful out there and safety can never be assumed. We would have been quite a victory for the Taliban if they hit such a number of our guys.

The call came in that the first Chinooks were inbound and as I knew I would be on the last one out I lined Buster up to say his goodbyes. Slowly a stream of lads came up and as they knelt down to stroke Buster there were more than a few teary eyes. I had only known these brave men for just over a month, but what a month it had been, and I considered them all good friends.

A smoke grenade was thrown and hissed out a steady stream of smoke, identifying the location of the helipad and indicating that it was safe to land. As a security measure the pilot is aware of the colour to expect. Everyone puts on their goggles as the Chinook's massive twin rotors throw dust and sand everywhere, which can be really painful if it hits you.

I ducked behind some Hesco and covered Buster as best I could. As I watched our friends the MERCIANs board this one I felt sad to see them go.

I didn't know then that the next time I would hear about the lads would be watching *Sky News* and learning about the death of Locky. He was tragically killed by a pressure pad IED on the last day of his third tour of Afghanistan. When Buster and I joined Locky and his men on foot patrol it was easy to see how respected he was as a friend as well as a leader of men. He would be sadly missed by everyone who knew him and served alongside him.

Our Chinook arrived and it was time to go. I leant over and checked Buster's harness and decided to leave it on him to make the transfer easier. That way I could get a grip on him and keep him secure. I wasn't sure how he would react as this was his first time on a Chinook and it was a different experience from flying with the Blackhawks. This time we walked up the ramp at the back, where the exhausts throw out massive blasts of hot air and the noise is huge. Buster wasn't bothered by any of it, which was a relief as I already had to carry my Bergan, day sack and weapon. Carrying a hysterical spaniel on top of it all would have been a nightmare.

As soon as I was on-board, my Bergan was thrown into the middle of the vastness and I was directed to a seat by the crewman. As I sat down the helicopter immediately started to rise. An Apache helicopter hovered above us to provide cover and deter attackers, but a carefully aimed rocket propelled grenade would have ruined everyone's day.

The Chinook threw us into our seats as it climbed rapidly, the engines squealing, even through our earplugs. The crewmen manned the machine guns at either end of the aircraft, alert and ready to lay down fire on any enemy activity. As for Buster, he had already found his way onto the seat next to me – unfortunately, a Chinook's seats are designed to collapse on any impact, so it was on the floor for him this time. I looked out of the window at the place that had been my home for the past month and had mixed feelings: relief at being out of there, memories of life-changing experiences and sadness because I had left some good friends. I suddenly felt very tired and looked down to see Buster sitting fast asleep with his head in my lap.

CHAPTER 8

Downtime

It was only a short journey over the desert, over the river, and then the main town of Gereshk passing below. As we started our descent I recognised the high watchtower of FOB Price and a few seconds later the crewman showed us a card with Price written on it. No point in talking as we wouldn't have heard a thing he said! We landed and quickly disembarked.

Although Price is relatively secure, it's still no place for a Chinook to idle so I picked up my Bergan and moved swiftly away so it could get off the ground again. The main helipad is tarmacked, but as soon as you step off it your boots hit loose aggregate which makes it hard going under foot. Luckily one of the movers grabbed my day sack to make life easier. Once clear of the landing area I could let Buster off his lead.

Despite having been away for a long time, he still remembered the post room and called in for a treat. After renewing old acquaintances we made our way to the kennels where it was a relief to take off my body armour and dump my bags. Buster, despite scoffing down a few biscuits a moment ago, was all pop eyed and padding about ready for his dinner, so I served up his non-rat pack meal and told him I would see him later.

'What???' He looked disgusted at me.

'See you later Buster,' was something he hadn't heard for several weeks. We had slept in the same mozzipod, shared every meal on camp and in the desert, worked together and played in the river. He had made me look clever and tried his best not to join in when I made a fool of myself. He had been my friend, my buddy and the 'person' closest to me throughout some pretty fearful times. No wonder he was upset with me. What he didn't know was that I was going to miss him too.

After leaving a very upset Buster in the kennels I made my way to the accommodation tent and had to fight the urge to climb straight into bed. When I say 'bed' it consisted of the same roll-up mat that we used with the mozzipod, but with two one-inch thick foam mats on top, rather than one. Not that comfortable, but when you're that tired, believe me, you will sleep on anything. I managed to hold out until I had taken a hot shower, shaved my head and had a proper shave. The showers are on a timer to save water and the idea is you get wet with the first lot, then lather up and then rinse it off with the second lot. That day I ignored the rules and was in there for a good five minutes, and a few minutes more cleaning the shower tray which seemed to have an inch of mud, sand and hair in the bottom. I changed into clean uniform and felt human again. Boy did it feel good.

The mess tent was calling me with tempting aromas and when I got there it all looked as good as I had imagined. I piled my plate high with fresh meat and vegetables – the things you miss the most on a rat pack diet – and launched into the man-size plateful, but could barely manage half of it before giving up. I remembered speaking to Mac when we were in The Fan and him telling me that when he went on R&R he promised himself all his favourite foods, but when faced with them he just wasn't hungry.

I didn't know what was going on with me but I knew someone who was always hungry so I put some of the meat in a serviette and headed back up to the kennels.

Buster greeted me as though he hadn't seen me for a week, jumping around like a whirling dervish in his kennel. I think it was me he was pleased to see, but chances are he was just as pleased to smell the roast meat in my pocket. I decided to spring him from his kennel so we could take a walk around the FOB, but the wander made me feel strangely empty so we cut it short and went back to the kennels. I sat down on the wooden bench and within seconds Buster was right next to me, head on my lap.

We sat together for a while and I told him how I was feeling and hoped he could make sense of it all because I was damned if I could. It felt like a no man's land of emotion: no high and no low, and nothing I was going to work through that night. I decided to take a leaf out of Buster's book and go to bed in the hope that things would be less fuzzy in the morning. I gave him a bit of a fuss and a scratch on his tummy and he opened one eye to check things out. 'Come on mate, it's time for bed. No mozzipod for us tonight but I'll be here first thing to get your breakfast and give you a run. Let's go now.'

Buster understood every word I said, I know he did, but he was used to having me as his pillow and I could see why the kennels didn't look quite so inviting. As I eased him off my lap I stood up and walked towards the gate. Buster had already made it past me and was sitting looking up at me, probably wondering where the hell I thought I was going. When I told him to get in his kennel, he just sat and stared at me. I felt so guilty, but in the end I had no choice but to pick him up and carry him in.

'OK it's not as comfy as the mozzipod and there's no one to cuddle up to, but you'll be fine. I promise you.'

I left him standing in the kennel and I could feel his eyes burning into the back of my head. I felt guilty and I hated leaving him.

I climbed into my bed, which was comfortable but strange. It was wonderful to be able to move my legs in my sleeping bag and to turn over when I wanted without having to negotiate a certain lump of spaniel. Having canvas rather than mozzipod between me and the sky, and no 81 mm mortars going off through the night, was good – but something was missing. I didn't sleep well at all.

I was up very early and headed straight to the Dog Section. Buster is a very clean dog who doesn't like to make a mess in his kennel so I always like to get to him early to let him out to do his business and enjoy a bit of morning exercise before I have a shower and breakfast. I received his usual excitable greeting, so I hoped that meant he had forgiven me for leaving him in the kennels overnight. I'm not sure if Buster had had a good kip or not. Funny how you can get used to be being trampled on in your sleep and then miss it when it's gone. We managed a lap of the base so he could let everyone know he was back in town and give them a chance to give him a fuss.

Without doubt Buster's favourite place on Price was the post room. There must have been three or four 'To a Dog in Afghanistan' boxes waiting for Buster to claim on his return. It was great to see.

In contrast, the morning visit was quite disheartening for me as my mail was following me around, and had missed me by a couple of days. I'm sure that there are still letters and parcels out there now trying to find me. No such problem for Buster though. His only problem was me being a miserable sod and rationing his treats.

Still, I was due my thirty-minute ration on the internet, which meant I could catch up on emails from home that had been building up over the past month. It would take several sessions to get through them all and to find out what was going on back in the real world. It was also nice to let people know that I was safe. Sitting at home, not knowing what was going on, is sometimes as hard as being there.

Afterwards, I took Buster into the Ops tent to let them know that we were back and ready for work but the place was in chaos with the MERCIANs packing up here too, again to let the Coldstream Guards move in. I made a phone call back to the Military Working Dogs Unit and was told to pack and be ready to move within the next two days.

I knew Buster wouldn't like my idea of a 'rest' so I decided it would do us both good to keep busy. Also, I didn't want Buster roaming around the base for a couple of days taking on a load of well-intentioned treats and snacks and then sleeping it all off courtesy of his mates in the watchtowers. I volunteered us for vehicle searches and when we weren't doing that I put Buster onto our explosive training sample kits to keep him at the top of his game. It was not just a matter of practising how to search but also a chance to remind him what it feels like to locate a 'find'. It's a bit like the buzz we get from a pat on the back from the boss: if you don't feel that buzz from time to time, then the job is not rewarding and it's not enjoyable. Buster needed to earn his reward, his tennis ball, and enjoy a really good play.

Give him his ball and he would run about with his half a tail stuck in the air and his head held high, growling when I tried to grab it from him. Buster's growl isn't threatening, it's just what he does, part of his character. If he goes into tail-wagging overdrive combined with his 'funny growl', that is the time to get concerned – that's when the game becomes work and takes on a serious edge. But when he's playing he's happy to drop the ball at my feet, and wait for me to throw it so he can bring it back to me ... he can go on for hours!

It was an uneventful two-day wait to move out but it was much-needed downtime, and I could tell that Buster was calmer and we were both ready to face the next challenge – whatever that turned out to be. Our bags packed, we headed to the helipad where our ride was due to land any moment. Absolutely on schedule the Chinook dropped in and quickly unloaded troops, mail and supplies. As soon as that was off, we boarded and took our seats. Buster was disgusted that, once again, he didn't have a seat and had to sit on the floor. As we started to rise the aircrew moved into position to man the guns, with the engines screaming to give us good height as fast as possible.

Looking over the back ramp we could see the ground flash by at a rate of knots, and flares being fired over potential hazardous areas. The flight back to Bastion is relatively short but it was still a relief to see the helipad below and the next batch of soldiers waiting to board. I attached Buster's lead to my webbing and picked up my bags. I was yet again reminded that it is not easy trying to carry all of your kit when you're attached to a spaniel who wants to go in a completely different direction.

I was happy to see the Dog Unit vehicle waiting for us, not least so I could lay down my equipment and take off my helmet, which was weighing really heavy. I knew the temperature was dropping a little but I wasn't feeling it. Buster was panting furiously but I guessed that was more down to excitement than heat. He was in a new place and there was every chance of making new friends. And that went for me as well.

There's a saying in the military: 'Pull up a sandbag'. It's when some of the lads want us to share stories from our tours, so in true *Jackanory* fashion (for those old enough to remember that BBC storytelling programme) the boys at Bastion had built a full armchair made from sandbags.

That evening, when it was my turn to speak, I sat in the big chair and told whoever would listen all about our time in the Green Zone – the highs and lows. Buster lay with his body over my feet and snored his way through it all. I'm glad he was there for what probably sounded like bedtime stories about Buster with a few bombs, bullets and a bit about me thrown in.

It was strange to see the lads who had not seen any action getting jealous of colleagues who had. The horror of it all didn't seem to matter. Yet I understood that, because the action is what we train for and how we need to test ourselves.

But as I told everyone: be careful what you wish for.

CHAPTER 9

Kabutlins

My orders for the next two days were to get our kit sorted and prepped to draft out. We were on the move – to Kabul. I was really excited about going because relatively few people get to see that part of the war, with most efforts concentrated on Helmand, the Taliban stronghold. After so many recent moves from camp to camp I had refined my packing skills to the point where I knew exactly what we needed for Buster, and the basics for me, so it took no time at all to put everything together.

So as not to appear idle, I volunteered Buster again to help the lads with vehicle searches on the main gate. This was not a popular decision with a certain hairy chap but all the same on the first morning Buster strutted happily ahead on the short walk from the unit to the gate. The only thing that stopped him in his jolly tracks was the sight of the vehicles all lined up, four abreast, ready for inspection. He took one look at them and then a long look back at me as if to say, 'Are you serious?'

I was serious, and he could see there was no way out of it, so we set to the job right away. Buster swaggered around the outside of the first vehicle and when he had finished that I lifted him onto the seat of the wagon so he could work his way through the cab and then through the middle. He was thorough and interested and by the time he had finished he was happy that it was clean – and we were reassured that the vehicle was good to go. Buster made this so easy and the locals who had nothing to hide were grateful for the dog's swiftness so they could get on and out.

A couple of hours later, just as I was lifting him into the next lorry – feeling myself getting all puffed up with pride at Buster's performance, and thinking of how I could get him a watery treat later for being the world's greatest search dog – he just flopped down on the driver's seat. It was our fourteenth vehicle search of the day and Buster had decided enough was enough.

Buster was on strike and I couldn't believe it. Not that he hadn't done this before, fourteen vehicles being his usual limit, but he hadn't completed the fourteenth yet! I fastened him to the Hesco Bastion wall and pretended to hide kit out, which meant giving him a chance to search with a guaranteed 'find' at the end of it, just to give him heart and renewed determination. This geed him up for another couple of wagons but that was it. He refused to jump into the next cab and when I lifted him in, he lay down on the cool seats.

I apologised to the lads for Buster downing tools, but they understood that once he decides he's had enough, that's it. In many ways it's a blessing that Buster is so strong-willed because it would have been dangerous to carry on when he was exhausted – although there is no doubt in my mind that he would still indicate on anything that was there, I'd have had to pull him off the job.

Very early the next morning, before sun-up, we were ready to move out to Kabul. Mike the patrol dog handler was picking us up to take us to the Flight Line, and like a good lad he had arrived early and kindly offered to exercise Buster and take him along. While he was doing this, I sorted our bags and loaded them and Buster's transit kennel onto a pallet.

There were only about a dozen of us on the flight and we waited together in the dark, donning our helmets, goggles and gloves, as the Hercules landed and rumbled to a standstill. It was so dark we couldn't see the plane until it was almost on top of us but once on the ground everything happened very quickly as usual: lights came on, the ramp lowered and personnel and kit were off-loaded. We followed our kit on-board and I set to coax Buster into his kennel.

The air loadmaster must have seen what I was up to and decided that Buster could sit on the seat next to me, which meant that he was also sitting next to a squadron leader doctor who said she was missing her own dogs very, very much. Buster was happy to stand in for her dogs and soak up the massive amount of fuss and kisses she landed on him. He gave her the full spaniel eyes, the special roll over and his famous Buster 'smile'. I ceased to exist for a while and that was fine. I was lucky to have one of my dogs with me in Afghan – that's the big perk in being a dog handler. I couldn't bear to be without Buster by now, so I knew where the doctor was coming from.

The engines levelled off so we got the order to remove body armour and helmets. It's always a massive relief, physically and mentally, to remove the protective gear and I was just enjoying the moment when the loadmaster approached me with a special request – could I take Buster into the cockpit to meet the crew? As if he had heard and understood the conversation Buster was on his feathery feet in no time and making his way up the steps to the flight deck.

He went instantly into his meet and greet routine, nuzzling up to each member of the crew in turn, lapping up all the attention. Then suddenly he stopped to eye-up a small cuddly toy sheep, sitting in pride of place in the cockpit, surrounded by photographs of the little mascot taken all over the globe. The co-pilot must have noticed Buster's interest in the toy and asked if he could take a photo of Buster holding it. 'No problem,' I said. Gently, in good gundog fashion, Buster took the toy from me and struck a regal pose giving it his best side with his head tilted and glistening snout in the air. It was all so picture perfect, until it all started to go wrong.

Buster had no intention of giving the sheep back. I should have seen that coming a mile off. As far as he was concerned, the little sheep had been given to him and was now his property. My problem was how to get the toy back, in one piece, without a fight, so I knew the first thing I needed was some edible bribery.

A quick whip-round produced a muesli bar which gave me some bargaining power: muesli bar for a toy sheep – simple. Clearly I'm as stupid as Buster sometimes thinks I am, because I should have guessed that he had only one plan and that was how to get the snack and keep the toy. His eyes were bulging as he looked at the muesli bar but he still maintained his vice-like grip on the sheep. There was a lot of looking at the snack bar, then at me, back to the snack before greed eventually got the better of him and he gave up the toy – a bit soggy but otherwise unharmed. I breathed a sigh of relief but the crew thought Buster was hilarious, a real comedian, with me as his perfect stooge. I didn't mind, as the episode earned us a place in the cockpit for the rest of the flight.

It was wonderful to have a pilot's view of Afghanistan spread far and wide beneath us. In the morning haze the mountain ranges around Kabul looked hauntingly mysterious and beautiful, and in the later sharp sunlight starkly rugged.

Then I had to pull myself away from the sightseeing to get Buster back down below for landing. It was time to don helmets and body armour again as we spiralled down to Kabul International Airport, or KIA NAPPA, as it's known among the British Troops. I grabbed my kit, which I appreciated was decidedly lighter than on my flight in, thanks to the fast-track desert training in what's really needed and what's a complete waste of space. The airport was relatively secure so the

Hercules was able to shut down its engines. The ramp went down and Buster said his goodbyes to everyone on-board. He had made a whole new set of friends in the space of a two-hour flight.

As we passed through the main part of the airport, Buster trotted along taking in all the new sights and sounds around him and I was pretty much doing the same. It was good to see an air of normality with locals booking in for flights with baggage and trolleys just like back home. The local airline livery was orange and you couldn't help but think of easyJet, although anyone going to Kabul on a stag night would be massively disappointed! Just in the airport the choice of restaurants and bars is a reflection of the different nations stationed there. The annoying thing for the British and American troops is that they can eat at the restaurants, but they are 'dry' to them. It's pretty much torture seeing others drinking alcohol with their meals – it really makes you want a beer!

I felt the drop in temperature from the moment we left the airport. It was definitely a few degrees cooler than Helmand, but I don't think Buster noticed and if he did he was would be as relieved as anyone wearing a fur coat. Just over the road I spotted a Saxon armoured vehicle, something that I hadn't seen since my days in Northern Ireland, and guessed it was our taxi to wherever we were off to next. I made my way over to be greeted by the crew, who loaded my kit into the vehicle and gave Buster a welcome pat and stroke. The only other passenger was the commanding officer of Camp Souter, our home for the next month or so. He was delighted to see Buster and made a real fuss of him too.

With Buster sitting calmly at my side, we set off on a twenty-minute journey through Kabul. He didn't seem to flinch at anything. I suppose he had seen and heard all of this before on his Bosnia tour, but for me it was a pretty lively journey and the noises were probably accentuated as we had been away from the bustle of city life for some time. Everything seemed loud and chaotic. The whole journey was punctuated with shouts and mini-flares being fired to maintain the security regulation that no vehicle is allowed within twenty metres of any convoy. It's due to the common risk of vehicle-borne suicide bombers and a good reason why all military vehicles display large, unmissable red signs on the back with the warning shown in words and pictures. Any vehicle ignoring the rule received a verbal warning first and a mini-flare followed. If they still came too close a volley of warning shots was fired. It was a tried and tested drill that proved successful and largely without incident. Sadly, the lads later told me there had been one tragic accident involving a man who had been shot – it turned out he was rushing just because he was late for work.

After twenty minutes the Saxon pulled up at Camp Souter and Buster and I piled out to be met by a crowd all there to welcome … Buster. We learned later that the talk of a new dog coming to camp had been buzzing for days. The first person to meet me was a Royal Army Veterinary Corps corporal dog handler called Simmo. He had been at Souter for a couple of months and was looking forward to moving on just for a change of scenery.

Simmo and his dog Kez, a black labrador, had been kept very busy and he filled me in on all the details as we made our way to the Dog Section, which, to my surprise, was brick built and with all the facilities we needed. The kennels were split in two, which included a comfortable sleeping area at the back for the dogs where they had both heating and air conditioning. I'm sure when Buster took a look around the facilities at Souter his first impression must have been something along the lines of: 'Bloody hell, it's the doggy Hilton!' And he would have been spot on. It was certainly a million miles away from sharing a cramped and often sweaty mozzipod with me.

Then I realised that the airport was only about 800 metres away. The reason for the long journey was to ensure that the route we took was always varied to minimise any attack on our patrols.

So he could give a first-hand review of his new home I put Buster in a kennel, which he really wasn't happy about. There was a bit of a stomping protest and the full-on sad eyes thing, but he forgave me the instant I gave him his tea a couple of minutes later. While Buster tucked in to his food I went with Simmo for a tour of the camp, which took no time at all. As we were enjoying a bit of boy banter about the dogs and the job to be done I was suddenly confronted by

Paula, a staff sergeant who said she had been waiting for days to meet Buster and was furious that I didn't have him with me!

Paula was a massive dog fan and kept a cupboard full of doggy treats that she got sent from the UK. Over the next month Paula and her colleague Bobbie, an RAF corporal, became Buster's best friends. It didn't take him long to learn the route to Paula's office or where she kept her treasure trove of treats.

Simmo took me over to our accommodation, another brick building with proper beds and showers. Believe me, after a spell in the desert just the thought of a real bed and shower was pure luxury. No wonder the place gained the nickname Kabutlins!

After dumping my bags, Simmo led the way to the mess hall where the excellent food was a far cry from rat-pack life in the Green Zone, and it set us up for the nightly brief at HQ attended by the heads of the relevant agencies.

Our brief for the following day was to work alongside the medical aid to civilian population (MEDCAP) exercise, which involved administering medicine to the locals. It was provided by the Americans and our job was to secure the area and provide Force Protection. And our protectors this time would be the Coldstream Guards.

Simmo had already checked out the compound chosen for the MEDCAP exercise and reckoned that it would take the two of us the best part of an hour to search the place. This would mean setting off from

Souter at around 0500 hours so with that in mind we went back to the section to take the dogs for a walk before bed. I put Buster back into his kennel and he gave me that now familiar withering look as if I was abandoning him rather than putting him to bed.

'Come on lad, it's not that bad. Look at the room you've got to spread out in. Compared to a mozzipod it's like having the penthouse suite! Get some sleep now Buster, we've got an early start lad and you have to be on top form.'

I gave him a good old fuss and he sloped off, head down, to his bed.

We were up but not very bright the next morning. We were ahead of sunrise and it was pretty cold out, so I grabbed a jacket before striding off to the kennels. Buster greeted me like a long lost friend with lots of jumping about. 'OK, OK Buster, that will do you noisy git. The rest of the place is asleep! There'll be no treats for you if you go and wake everyone at dawn. Come on let's go for a quick walk.'

While I was talking Buster into getting his act together, I was mentally sorting what I needed and wondering how the day would go. It would be a new experience for me, although it was still searching, and Buster looked ready for a full day.

It would be good to work with Simmo and having both dogs on duty. After a quick jog around the storage area with Buster, I put my body armour on and gathered my kit before taking the short walk to the main gate. Weapons were signed out and checked and Buster made his presence felt among his new friends. His full 'spaniel eyes' trick and sly sniffing of pockets and kit didn't earn him any treats, but the lads had a lot on their minds. Buster's presence did what it always did – it broke the tension and brought a smile to a few faces. It's amazing the calming effect that can have on a group of anxious people and Buster did it everywhere he went. I've always thought that was one of his very special qualities.

As we approached the main gate I saw the vehicles all lined up in preparation for a couple of immediate action drills. It's what we were expecting ahead of the operation. The drills were essential to ensure that everyone knew exactly what to do if we came under attack, and this included what the lads would have to do with Buster if I got injured, or killed. If you allowed yourself to think about it too much, the drills were very sobering: a reminder of the worst that could possibly happen, that not everyone comes home.

The drill went well and Buster carried out his duties – being in the right place at the right time – perfectly, which seemed to reassure the lads.

We were ready to enter the centre of Kabul.

Sat in the back of a Snatch you can't see anything but you can hear lots of shouting, blasting of horns and mini-flares being fired. We were very cramped so Buster had to sit on my knee. After a short while we arrived at the compound which appeared to be a building full of offices that had either been abandoned or half refurbished.

The potential problem on this operation was that the MEDCAP had been widely publicised, making the threat of an IED being planted very real indeed. Our concern was that in addition to the military there would be a high number of civilians there too, including children and elderly members of the community in need of basic healthcare. This would be a big hit for the insurgents.

Simmo and I had already formulated a search plan and made everyone aware of who would be where and when. We had to make sure that everywhere had been checked and no one was allowed anywhere until we had been there first. And as an extra layer of security we were given a 'cover man' to look out for us and to point out any areas that we may have missed. My cover man was the company sergeant major, he was an excellent soldier and a great bloke to boot. He was about six feet tall with dark hair and an athletic build. Being in Kabul, like everyone else he was clean shaven and freshly laundered. He was very interested in what we had done in the Green Zone and a bit jealous of not having had a chance to go down there himself.

But there was no less danger in the kind of search we were about to take on. It's still searching without knowing what's around the corner – literally. Buster was excited and up for the challenge, and one look at his eager face and bright eyes was as good as hearing someone say, 'It will be OK … if we just get on with it, everything will be OK.' His confidence rubbed off on me and I was silently grateful. We had a search plan and not much time to work through it, so we got going with Buster bustling forward weaving in and around all the exterior walls before setting a paw indoors.

As we worked our way around, it was evident that this was a massive site with out-houses, gardens and all manner of rummage areas. A bit more time would have been very useful, but we had to get it done before the Americans arrived. Buster worked like a dream and I dread to think how long the search would have taken without him and Kez on the job. Human beings just can't work as thoroughly or as quickly as a dog. And no one can be trusted more than a dog.

Once the exterior was finished, we split the interior between the two animals. The building was never-ending! It had three floors, but then we discovered we had an attic and a cellar to make safe too. Buster needed to be at the top of his game, so I made sure that he was taking on plenty of water and taking short rests in between the rooms.

I needn't have worried. Buster was loving this challenge, with every room presenting new smells and interest. It was a pleasure to see him work and be so sure-footed. It was a massive relief when the dogs had finished and I think everyone felt they could relax, to some extent at least.

Now the site was clear, our snipers were deployed onto the roof and the gates were guarded so each visitor could be searched before entering. Our positioning wasn't great – the site was at the side of a dual carriageway, so one half had been blocked off to reduce the possibility of a suicide vehicle threat. Our Snatch Land Rovers did a great job of being a road block until the Americans arrived with their own brand of very scary armoured vehicles. I went around the back of the building to catch up with our transport and found two very tall Guardsmen standing right by it. One of the guys, Chris, introduced himself but the others spotted Buster pottering along by my side and immediately stooped down to make a fuss of him – while he moved in on their butty boxes.

Both dogs had done a great job and deserved to relax a little. It felt safe enough for us to relax a little too, and take off our helmets and don our floppy hats. It was regarded as a 'hearts and minds' exercise so we didn't want to look too aggressive, which isn't easy when you consider the amount of firepower we carry. When the American forces arrived there wasn't a floppy hat in sight. It was all helmets and sunglasses.

By the time we were ready to open the gates the sun was baking hot. We made a last search of the gate area before it was opened to the local people, who were turning up in droves. Word had successfully spread and the Guardsmen were fully occupied checking everyone through as fast and as safely as possible. It seemed like the whole of Kabul had turned out, as well as visitors from further afield. Buster was in his element with new soldier friends making a fuss of him and a whole load of other people he just might want to mingle with too. The usual routine of telling the guys not to feed him or throw things for him was soon ignored, and the look on Simmo's face told me that he had been through all this long before I arrived.

The crowds kept coming and there were some incredible sights to behold. Entire families were making an outing of it, with young and old packed into vehicles of all sizes. Determined not to miss out on treatment for his grandmother, a young boy, I'd say no older than ten years old, brought the old lady along in a wheelbarrow. As the crowds grew, the queue jumping and swapping sparked a number of disturbances that looked likely to get out of hand. People arguing wasn't a major problem but the chaos could turn into a security risk so the decision was taken to break out our best security measure – our dogs.

Buster and I joined Simmo and Kez to peacefully part the crowds by walking between them. As if by magic, we suddenly had two very quiet, well-behaved lines of people, just sat staring at us. Well, to be more accurate, staring at the dogs. Simmo and I couldn't help laughing only because the dogs looked so proud of themselves. Buster was puffing out his chest, which made him look extra regal as he strutted along. I thought he was probably imagining himself as a patrol dog.

Once order had been restored we discovered that walking the dogs around was enough to maintain the peace. Not surprisingly, some of the people were scared but many more were just fascinated by Buster, and I noticed some people daring others to stroke him as he walked past. Once a couple had reached out to him everyone seemed to want to touch him, much to his delight.

I think he was disappointed with the lack of food from this particular crowd though. He made some brave attempts to sniff and search pockets and sacks but there wasn't anything there. It had been a very long day and the luxuries that awaited us back at Souter pressed heavy on my mind. The showers, good food and the real bed were going to be very welcome after a full-on day with our American friends doling out healthcare to the masses.

Packed like sardines in the back of the Snatch on the way back to base meant that Buster was back on my lap. After spending the whole day with the Guardsmen, making new friends and getting praise for his good work, I was very happy that it was my lap Buster chose to slump onto, then dribble and fall asleep. I gave him a big pat and ear ruffling to say 'thank you mate'.

CHAPTER 10

Dangerous Days

Souter looked very inviting and after dropping Buster into the kennels I left him tucking into his tea before heading to the mess to tuck into mine. After that it was off to O Group and to a sobering announcement: the following morning I would be patrolling Buster along the Jalalabad Road.

At the time, the road had the dubious honour of being the most bombed road in the world. The main danger came from suicide bombs, which were now commonplace. Several American patrols had fallen foul to this threat. Just weeks after our tour ended, a British Saxon was blown up, killing all on-board.

It was another cold, early morning start but Buster was happy to leave the comfort of his heated kennel and let off steam, running around the camp while all was still quiet. After that it was time to pack our kit and take a walk down to the Guardroom. Weapons were made ready and we mounted up in the vehicles ready for our journey.

There are times in a search dog handler's career when you fear complacency. In the UK, when you are searching the same venue week in week out, you often have to give yourself a kick up the backside to remind yourself why you are there. However, when it's your job to search and make safe stretches of the most dangerous road in the world, complacency doesn't enter the vocab.

There's a rule out there – every vehicle and every person is a potential threat. I had no problem keeping that at the forefront of my mind. My throat was dry and I was drinking large amounts of water even before we reached the drop-off point. We dismounted from the Snatch Land Rovers and everyone checked their own equipment. It was just me and Buster on the road, with the two vehicles driving behind, ready to give covering fire if we needed it.

When we reached the chosen search point on this 95-mile stretch of road that links Kabul with Jalalabad, the largest city in eastern Afghanistan, I was very much aware that this was a very busy road. I needed to make sure that Buster was never far from me or too near the traffic. But few people were around in the early hours to interfere with what we were doing and Buster was on form – his nose in the air sifting the smells of the morning from the smells on the ground that he knew to be dangerous.

As we worked the roadside, checking primarily for IEDs, we saw the city come to life. On the outskirts of the capital we could see plenty of activity, with domestic fires being set and freshly baked bread and breakfast aromas drifting on the air. There were domestic smells of all kinds, in fact; some so horrid you really couldn't place them. The stench from the many open sewers in the city was beyond belief.

As the search wore on, the volume of traffic increased, although I could never work out where the people were going. In cars, wagons and vans, with their belongings piled high on top, there was a constant migration of people travelling ... somewhere.

It was getting very busy so I decided to keep Buster on a long line, and that was for a couple of good reasons: first to prevent anyone grabbing and running off with him; and, of course, to keep him away from the road. Buster is an amazing search dog, and I was always happy to put my life in his paws every day, but he has absolutely no road sense whatsoever. We talk about the Green Cross Code (and the Tufty Club if you are of a certain age) but Buster hasn't a clue and that's because when he's working he is concentrating on his job, selecting clues from the many varied scents.

Keeping close to Buster was a must to keep him safe and away from the roadside, but it had its own problems. If Buster indicated a 'find' I would be right on top of the thing too. Knowing that you are searching such a dangerous road for explosive devices is enough to keep you mentally alert, but when it was over I would be mentally drained, too. Handlers are always looking for a change in their dog's behaviour and this can happen when they pass over something and then trot back to check it again or just do a 'check step' – which is when the head stops, but the body carries on past. Usually it's just them being a dog and you can send them on with a quick command. However when you are on a long line, every movement is exaggerated.

On the Jalalabad Road, every time Buster stopped or whipped his head around, my heart skipped a beat. I had a sneaking suspicion that by the end of the search he was probably doing a funny little check step here and there just for his own amusement!

The day searching the road was more than a routine search, it was also a chance to chat to the local people. It was all well-intentioned but it was not always well received.The expressions on the locals' faces was usually enough to let us know if we were going to be offered a cup of tea and a slice of hospitality or not.Today, hostility was in all their eyes. But once again Buster's ability to become a clown when it was needed paid off.

We don't usually like people interfering with our dogs when they are working but in these circumstances I was happy to let some of the children stroke him and make friends. He played to their giggles and they loved it. At the same time I stayed well aware of what was going on around us and wasn't going to be fooled into a false sense of security. A search dog of Buster's calibre would be worth a great deal to a Taliban group as a trophy, they may even want a ransom. He was worth more to me than that, so I needed to keep my wits about me.

By the time we had finished the search and got back to the Snatch I was exhausted from the pure concentration. My clothes were drenched and it wasn't particularly hot. Buster was just glad to be off the lead and he slumped down on the floor of the vehicle so I knew he felt the same as me. At the time I felt safe in the back of the Land Rover but looking back it wouldn't have taken much to blow us all up. Ignorance is sometimes bliss.

After a rest and a clean-up of the kennels, I reached for Buster and went for a wander around the camp. We hadn't gone far when we ran into our company sergeant major, who told me that we were down to join a patrol around the Russian Flats later on that afternoon. He had a warning for me too: syringes, and lots of them, lying on the ground. This had to be the opportunity to try Buster in his boots.

Although he had worn them in training, I'd never used them in the field so he would need a bit of a refresher at least. The little cloth and rubber booties are great for protecting a dog's paws from sharp mental or glass and extremely hot or cold surfaces. The dogs who searched Ground Zero after the 9/11 terrorist attacks wore the boots – but they are not for every dog and can be an acquired taste. Buster decided very quickly that they were not for him.

Just bringing the boots out of their pouch was enough for Buster. First he thought it was something to eat and was interested and then he discovered it wasn't food and changed his mind.

'Boots Buster, that's all they are, and if our man is right about the syringes then you'll be glad of these later on.'

He sat and listened to me.

'Paw! Buster give me your bloody paw!' As if his paws were glued to the ground, Buster sat like a statue, head up and avoiding my gaze. What followed can only be described as a wrestle and I think I won.

I wish I had taken a video of Buster in boots, it was hilarious. I threw his ball and off he went after it. It was like asking someone to run in flippers. The sight of him with his legs flinging all over the place soon drew a crowd and the lads stood around watching were in stitches. Poor Buster, it was not his finest hour. He needed a few more training sessions before we tried that one again. This time, he would have to rely on me to look out for him and the syringes or anything else that could do him harm.

By the time the 'dogs in boots' jokes were shared and all the hilarity had died down, it was time to collect our kit and head for the Guardroom to sign out our weapons. We were with a new set of lads, so Buster enjoyed the introductions and the fuss that goes with being an instant star. Everyone in the new unit was happy to hear they would have a dog along on the patrol and Danni, a Royal Military Policewoman assigned to the unit, was so impressed with Buster that she later transferred to the RAVC. She was all over him and Buster was all over her – possibly something to do with her being one of those special people who could always magic a biscuit from nowhere.

Another cramped trip in the back of a Snatch was on the cards but this time it was going to be a real mystery tour. Buster was fine and happy with his new friends so my head started to concentrate on the noises coming from inside and outside the vehicle.

There were some now-familiar sounds of the lads doing top cover shouting to passers-by to keep their distance, and the occasional release of a mini-flare when the shouts were ignored, but it was still frustrating not being able to see what was going on. I had volunteered to do top cover but the amount of extra body armour needed for the job would have been restrictive during the searches, so I didn't get the chance in Kabul. When we came to a halt I correctly assumed we had reached the Flats. We had planned to run a drill as soon as we got there so we all dismounted and got into position.

The Flats were horrible. A sprawling mass of run down and half-crumbled Afghan buildings, and between the ruins little 'villages' had sprung up randomly out of the poverty, made up of home-crafted huts with tin roofs. It was a filthy and run-down place, and home to junkies, refugees and anyone who wanted to fall off life's radar. This was one place where Buster would not be making friends.

The lads on top cover had their eyes constantly to their rifle sights scanning the roofs and windows for threats, because this was exactly the kind of place where weapons or explosives were likely to be hidden by the Taliban. There were just so many places to hide the dangers and the poor residents were highly unlikely to talk to the authorities. The community was too afraid and much too tightly knit for any of that.

As I fixed Buster into his harness I told him to be careful, 'Buster, we need to get this job done and get out of here as soon as possible.'

I'm sure he nodded his silky head. This was not a good place to be and I based that not just on what I could see but also how vulnerable I felt. It's stupid to go into a place if you don't have somewhere to escape to, so before we started I memorised a safe escape route out, should anything go wrong. I tugged on Buster's harness and reassured myself it was secure: 'You're ready to go, mate. Don't worry, I'm right behind you.'

On occasions, when we had to search around the back of buildings, it wasn't uncommon to discover open toilets. The putrid smell was overpowering along with the drone of the flies that went with them. I tried hard not to wretch at every step. I wished I could have held my nose but I needed both hands for Buster: one to hold his lead and the other free in case I needed to use my weapon. Buster, despite his heightened sense of smell, just carried on regardless, as if we were walking through a bed of roses. I needed to sideline the smell too but I couldn't help wondering how people managed to live like this day after day.

The Russian Flats cover a huge area but we could only search small sections at a time. Buster was nose up and concentrating right away and I was encouraging him along as it wasn't an area we wanted to hang around in. It would have been easy for the Taliban to set up an ambush and if they were watching us they could see we weren't out in massive force. Buster was working well despite a few distractions, sometimes syringes and broken glass, but mostly other animals. Feral dogs and cats were a big problem and I had to rely on some of the lads to scare them away before they crossed Buster's search path. Sometimes the guys had to use mini-flares, which was great and no one was harmed, but sometimes whoever was popping the flare forgot to warn the rest of us, and we ended up with rifles pointed in all directions.

We didn't wait around, twenty minutes tops, and headed out breathing a sigh of relief. For the second time that day I felt shattered, and Buster was soon asleep on my feet on the floor of the Snatch. Not much was said on the way back but Buster got plenty of strokes even though he was oblivious to it all.

When we reached camp I had to wake Buster from a deep sleep, which was unusual – a big indication that the search of the Flats had been mentally as well as physically exhausting.

'Buster, Buster, come on lad let's go.' I was leaning over him and stroking his ears as I spoke to him, and I'm sure he would have carried on snoozing if I hadn't given him a prod.

He stood up and gave himself such a big shake that he nearly shook himself off his feet. Then a big stretch and a yawn followed before he decided to leave the vehicle. Until we stepped out I hadn't realised that Buster's fan club was waiting to see him. The lads and Danni took it in turns to stroke the bomb dog who they said kept them safe that afternoon. It was great to watch him get all the fuss he deserved and I knew I would have a chance to thank him properly later for his part in keeping me safe that day.

For now the best I could do was let him lead the way to stores and his biscuit cupboard. Paula and Bobbie gave him the biggest hug. It seemed that Buster had found his captive audience and all was well in his world.

CHAPTER 11

Buster the Talisman

Souter was a strange camp and one of the oddest things about it was the variety of shops run by locals. They sold what can only be described as an eclectic mix of things, including electrical goods, DVDs and local crafts. There was also a tailor, who came highly recommended for his skill and value for money, so I decided to pay him a visit. It had been a long time since I had needed or bought a suit but I thought it would be a good time to have one, especially on the cheap. I had to leave Buster behind – not that he minded as I left him with Paula and Bobbie, who spoilt him to death the moment my back was turned.

The tailor's shop was very small, very dingy and packed to the ceiling with bolts of material of all colours and weights. When I told the man what I wanted I was given a Next catalogue for my style guide followed by a pile of swatches to choose the material. I was measured up and four days later I was the proud owner of a made-to-measure three-piece suit that cost me $70.

The waistcoat had a silk back in the colours of the RAF Police 'Mars Bars' and the workmanship was faultless. Of all the things that I expected to bring back from a war, a three-piece suit was not one of them. The great thing is, I've still got it and it still fits, despite me being several pounds lighter out there. I also had a flag made with Buster's name and mine, beside a picture of Buster that one of the lads from the MERCIANs had drawn for me. I flew that flag on all of the kennels that we went to after that. It's still one of my treasures from my time there.

As well as the shops there was a weekly market where other locals would set up stalls selling an even more incredible selection of things, including sunglasses, carpets, pashminas and cheap souvenirs.

It was Buster's job to search the gymnasium where the market was held before it was set up in the morning. We then had to go straight out to the gate to search the vehicles bringing the goods in. The market was seen as a potential easy cover for trafficking trouble in and out of the camp, so Buster's presence was invaluable.

One morning's search was going along really well – Buster was swaggering along happily, clearing the vehicles and the people entering the camp with their wares, when suddenly he stopped and went into his famous 'growl and dance' routine. I immediately shouted, 'Find!' and everyone went into defensive positions. Fortunately, our friend Chris the guardsman was on hand and recognised the man standing by the 'suspect' goods. He was a man who brought antique and replica weapons to market, so Buster was right on the button sniffing him out, but just to be sure he didn't have anything else in his boxes he was asked to open everything he was carrying. It really was a great collection and he obviously looked after his weapons a lot better than most Afghanis, but antiques or not, this was still a weapons 'find' for Buster so I rewarded him with his ball.

Of course this became a weekly routine for Buster, and we never could take a chance. Every week, once the vehicles were in, the locals would set up their stalls and then have to leave the gym for the search. Buster would always do a full search and end with the antique weapons guy indicating a 'find', and I would always reward him with his ball. All this was probably a pain for the stall holders and the punters, but it gave me the opportunity to spot any early bargains before the market opened! The added perk for Buster was that when he headed out of the gym he could dodge through the door leading direct to Supplies where Paula would dish out his daily treat!

The weapons guy really had an impressive range of homemade military equipment – holsters, webbing belts and antique muskets. I was tempted by the muskets and bought two, one for me and one for my brother – and had them 'gift wrapped' – as a Christmas present for him. I remember handing him the box and him saying, jokingly, 'I hope this isn't an AK-47?' Which was quite a question as he is a civilian police firearms officer! When he opened the box he was confronted with the stock of a rifle and looked very pale until, with great relief, he revealed the muskets.

Buster loved to search in real time and he loved to practise too. He didn't mind one way or another because for him the outcome was always the same: success equals a chance to play with his ball. Our 'down' days were devoted to training searches and I found the Guardsmen were always up for a bit of fun where Buster was concerned. I would ask one of the lads to hide some training explosive within the camp and then let Buster dash off to find it. 'Beat Buster' became a favourite game on camp and I was always amazed how inventive the lads could be with their hiding places. It was a popular talking point at mealtimes, with the soldiers discussing where they had hidden stuff and where they were going to try next to out-do Buster! The only times they succeeded in beating him was when they chose ridiculous hiding places that he couldn't possibly reach. I guess being beaten by a dog every time can get a bit frustrating.

We had been in Afghanistan two months when we were given a very emotive task. We were asked to search a cemetery in the centre of Kabul ahead of a visit from the British ambassador for Remembrance Sunday. That's all we knew at first, but when we got there it turned out to be a cemetery for British servicemen killed in previous conflicts in the region. It was a very poignant reminder that we had never won a war in this country.

It was a small and underwhelming site, a walled compound with just a small wooden sign saying 'British Cemetery', but inside the grounds were immaculate and a real tribute to the individuals who tended it. I felt respect for the Afghanis that this memorial had never been desecrated.

After Buster had conducted the search we locked down the area and awaited the arrival of the British ambassador and several high ranking British and foreign officials. We stayed for the service of remembrance and then made our way back to Souter for our own service. As the list of fallen soldiers' names were read out, name after name, I looked around the room and most of my colleagues were wiping tears off their cheeks.

Over the next few days I saw something that I didn't expect to see in the desert – snow! It was so strange, especially as it wasn't even snowing in the UK. Buster loved it and I'd never seen him in snow before so it was a treat for me too. He even got involved in a mass snowball fight with the lads. There were snowballs flying everywhere and he was loving it – but I was not. I know a lot of people thought I was being miserable not wanting Buster to play, or that I was being huffy because he was ignoring me. The problem was, it may have been a snowball fight to the soldiers but to Buster it was still playing with a 'ball', and he only got to do that as a reward when he was working. Playing 'ball' like this was sending him mixed messages, so I had to call him out of the game and take him back to the kennels. I stayed with him for a while, explained my actions, dried him off and made sure he was warm.

'Come on, you bloody idiot, you'll catch your death out there.'

I suddenly thought what a stupid thing to say to a dog who faces the threat of bullets and bombs every day!

The weather never hindered what we had to do in Afghan, but snow and rain put a whole new complexion on the land. When the sand got wet it turned to mud, a grey sticky kind that plastered everything and everyone. Buster didn't mind the weather or where the job took us, as long as I was around and I wasn't too mean on the food. One thing I'm sure he found confusing about meeting the locals was the lack of treats on offer when we did community work. To me this was a blessing, as I would have had to put a stop to it even though it was often Buster's presence that lowered the tension and hostility.

The locals on our doorstep who lived in the compounds on the perimeter of Souter were familiar with the comings and goings of our troops, so we really needed them on our side. Local intelligence from this source was vital and for that we needed to gain and maintain a relationship, and this is where Buster came into his own. No one seemed to notice the mud on our boots or the full body armour because Buster turned out to be the man of the moment. As we searched and chatted to the locals, we soon had a long trail of children in tow – like a canine Pied Piper, Buster drew in his crowd and entertained them. Anyone looking on would have wondered how on earth a spaniel from the UK could do so much for the 'hearts and minds' operation by just being himself. But then that's the magic of Buster.

Not to be left out, the Coldstream Guards devised a goodwill plan of their own. The regiment is largely recruited from the North East of England, so they persuaded Newcastle United to send them a consignment of football shirts which they handed out to some of the football-mad locals. I joked with them, 'Bloody hell lads, don't you think these people have it bad enough as it is without having to wear those shirts?' But of course I actually thought it was a great idea.

The Taliban threat is ever-present but cleverly hidden in the weave of everyday life. When word reached us that a gang of insurgents was hiding out in a compound just beyond our area of responsibility it brought the threat to our door. Local intelligence had unearthed enough for us to move in on them but Buster and I would be there to provide the necessary cover, searching for hidden weapons and explosives.

The camp was buzzing with the same level of excitement we saw in the Green Zone, and the Coldstream Guards were itching for a chance to get stuck into some action against the enemy.

I packed quickly and then checked my weapons and ammo to make sure everything was serviceable and clean. I took the rounds out of my magazine and dusted everything off to ensure the springs still worked and that there was no dust to go down the barrel of my rifle. I checked that I had spare batteries for everything and it's amazing how many different types of battery that you need – some of them special ones, like for your laser light module. This is a great bit of kit that fixes to your rifle. It is a torch and a laser sight that can enable you to get shots off quickly in close quarters at night. It can also be used in infrared mode with night vision goggles.

Everything was ready. I just need to explain to Buster what was going on and to give him his meal before we both turned in for an early night. He was pleased to see me appear at the kennel door and I gave him a really big hug. I'm not sure if he sensed something in me or not but when I knelt down to him he snuggled into me and just let me hold him.

'Good lad, Buster. Looks like we're going to see some action tomorrow, so you need your beauty sleep, mate.'

I didn't know what we would be facing, no one did, but a dawn raid on the enemy was bound to end in an exchange of bullets.

'Don't worry Buster, I'm not going to let you out of my sight.'

He looked up at me and narrowed his eyes as I stroked his head. He understood.

I went to the block, had a shower and watched a DVD. Although I intended to have an early night the adrenaline was already pumping and sleep was hard to catch. I must have nodded off, though, because the next thing I heard was my alarm.

I was up before anyone else started to stir as I needed to get Buster sorted and then double-check our equipment. It was still dark as I walked to the Guardroom where the lads were already waiting.

They were all hyped-up and eager to get their hands on Buster – not just to fuss him this time, but because everyone wanted him in their wagon.

Buster had become something of a lucky talisman so there was going to be a fight over him unless someone had a plan to assign him to a particular group. I think the company sergeant major saw what was going on and assigned me to a call-sign, leaving the rest of them well miffed as if they had forgotten we were all going to the same place.

We all piled into the vehicles and Buster managed to grab a seat, so he was happy. The second the last man took his seat the Snatch shot off at speed. We didn't have time to waste. We wanted to surprise the Taliban and hit them before they had time to think, never mind pick up a weapon.

Once out of the city we were surrounded by the dark shadows of the mountains, and now we had to blend with the night too. All vehicle lights were extinguished and our night vision goggles came into play. We inhabited a very small and dark world where the trusted eyes and ears of the top cover guys were our guides.

The road was nothing more than a dirt track with a sheer drop on the one side. I breathed a sigh of relief when we reached the relative cosiness of the harbour area and quickly jumped out of the vehicle. It was then I noticed how young most of the lads were. They were full of enthusiastic banter, so keen to go and collect some battle scars, and I thought to myself, My God, they think they're invincible. Buster sensed my mood and mirrored it. We all needed his sensible side right now. The boisterous soldiers were enough without having a ditzy dog along too. But it didn't take the lads too long to realise that we were now in the danger zone.

The plan was for me to lead the way with Buster, clearing the route for the lads to follow. I harnessed Buster up and set off, saying goodbye to the men who would be staying with the wagons – much to their disgust. The preparation had taken longer than expected and the sun was beginning to come up, which for me was good as I could work Buster without my night vision goggles.

When we reached our prepared laying-up point we went to ground, catching a glimpse of the compound we were going to attack. I could feel the excitement around me as everyone readied their personal weapons and the more specialist weapons were broken out. Unlike Helmand, we didn't have the added assurance of the Vikings' extra heavy firepower and that was a shame. It always felt safer with them around.

We started our way down towards the compound when the order come down to, 'Go to ground!'

We all stopped and took up defensive positions. My heart was pounding as I laid my hand on Buster's back to steady him and keep us both low to the Afghan soil. We could hear what was going on over the radios – and clearly something was happening that we troops hadn't expected. As we sat and watched, hunkered down on the ground, two American Apache helicopters flew overhead. Large cheers then went up as the Apaches struck home in spectacular form with their own brand of firepower, destroying the compound on our behalf.

It was galling to watch the Americans step in. But if the Apaches were used it was serious, and going in as planned might have left us a few lads short. I was suddenly very aware that Buster and I had been due to be the first ones in.

As we made our way back to Souter in a quieter mood, I could hear the lads talking about their disappointment and how they were ready for a piece of the action. I can't say I shared this feeling. But I had to smile at the bravado of the lads and their declarations of how they would have taken the Taliban apart, given the chance. I never doubted them.

When we arrived back at camp and downloaded our weapons, before a debrief in fifteen minutes. I took Buster to the kennels and gave him a well-deserved treat and a cuddle, and promised to be back later. During the brief we were informed that, as it was light when we arrived, as a precaution the Americans had sent up an unmanned aerial vehicle to look at the compound.

It transpired that the earlier intelligence we had received was horribly inaccurate. The number of Taliban in there greatly exceeded what we were expecting and our arrival was not going to be a surprise. They had amassed some heavy weapons of their own and were preparing to use them. On this occasion it was God Bless America.

I went back to the kennels and sat with Buster, telling him all about the debrief and how glad I was to be back and to be alive. As usual he sat and listened and took it all in his stride. Just sitting with him was important to me and as I stroked him I was well aware that the moment could have been so different – even non-existent.

After about an hour I went to check my emails and found one from Tracy, in Iraq. I wanted to talk to her so much right then, but her email saying how much she loved and missed me was a massive boost. I needed that because the rest of my tired mind was concentrating on how precious life is. I was asking myself just what was I was doing at over forty years old, still running around like a kid with a gun.

You can always rely on the Forces to cheer you up though. As I was trying to magic-up a moment with Tracy and imagine what she would say to me, I noticed the guardsman sitting down from me checking his emails was doing his nut. His ex-girlfriend had gone onto his Facebook account, changed his status to homosexual and posted all manner of demeaning details, and then changed his password so he couldn't go in and alter it. Now that must have topped off his already shit day.

I went back to the kennels and took Buster for a walk. He had worked hard, and so I took him (or maybe he took me) to Supplies and to his treat cupboard, then we went to my room and watched a DVD together. I let him stay, and for once his snoring was music to my ears.

CHAPTER 12

Working with Uncle Sam

There were so many times while we were in Afghan that I thanked God for Buster. Every day we worked together he made me want to be a better dog handler, because he was such a special dog. As our tour progressed, the strain of having to be vigilant and aware of potential dangers every minute of every day was starting to tell on me. I was luckier than most, because I could call on Buster's strength when my own reserves were low. Even when he was under pressure he was still helping me. He just kept on giving and giving.

Towards the end of our time in Kabul we were deployed to a night patrol in the mountains. The Snatch was our workhorse in those days, wherever we had to go that was almost always our mode of transport. The rugged hills that rise up around Kabul are, in the main, unknown territory and hold secrets of their own.

We had just started on a steep uphill track when the driver shouted: 'Top cover down!' The two cover guys immediately dropped down alongside me and Buster as the engine revved crazily and we lurched forward. Buster launched himself onto my knee and we both turned to look through the small back window to see if we were under attack.

I couldn't see a thing but it felt as if we were in an aircraft taking off, with the bottom of the hill disappearing into a small, black speck. I didn't know how far we had to go, but I knew I wanted this to stop. We were going uphill at a rate of knots with the revs falling away rapidly. I held on to Buster.

'It's OK mate, we'll be OK. I'm not going to let you go. Trust me.'

Buster looked at me as if to say: 'Are you sure?'

I was sure, but the gradient of the track was now almost vertical and we were still climbing in the dark. I think the driver just wanted to get us to the top without attracting attention from the Taliban.

Buster must have sensed I was flapping and tried to get even further up my body to cover me. With Buster now standing on my legs and with his head next to mine, the Snatch seemed to level out and we slid to a halt. We all got out and looked down the hill that we had climbed at breakneck speed. Fair play to the driver for getting us up there, but one little mistake or another couple of hundred metres further to go up, and I'm not sure that we would have made it. Falling off the side of a mountain in Snatch Land Rover, 4,000 miles from home, was not how I wanted it all to end for me or for Buster. I was angry about the 'what could have happened' and it all seemed more poignant as we were so close to the end of this part of our tour.

*

Working with the American forces in Afghan always gave me a chance to show off Buster's search skills. He was now well-known by the Brits, Danes and other strands of the NATO Forces, thanks to the regiments we had worked with in Helmand and then Kabul, and to have the Americans singing his praises too felt really good. As it happened, our last big operation in Kabul was another MEDCAP, this time just outside Camp Phoenix, an American base in the centre of the city.

A unit carried out a recce a couple of days before the planned date, just so I could get it clear in my head about how best to secure the area. After our previous medical programme experience, I knew we would be clearing the area for arms and explosives, and then acting as crowd control too.

When we drove into the camp I could not believe my eyes. The place had lots of shops and so many different eating outlets that it was more like a slice of New York than Kabul. I've heard it said that the Americans can't go to war without street lighting and Burger King, and this certainly seemed to confirm the rumour.

The place chosen for the MEDCAP was an abandoned building just beyond the perimeter wall of the camp and, although covered by the American watchtower, I still wanted to make sure it was 'Buster clean'. It was not a nice place and had obviously been a hangout for drug users. The evidence was everywhere. I wanted the syringes and the rest of the shit cleared out before I took Buster in there, but this was out of the question as there was a serious risk of

IEDs being present – which of course was why Buster was needed. I wasn't in the mood to take too many risks with my dog, he had faced enough already and it was my job to protect him and get him home in one piece. After speaking to Steve, the captain in charge, and getting his word that at least the outside of the place would be cleared for Buster to search, we made our way back to the camp and decided to stay for something to eat.

Like kids in a sweetshop the lads scanned the tasty choices on offer and skipped off in various directions to get their pizza or Chinese or burgers. One of our number recommended the BBQ, so I went for that and for a couple of dollars feasted on burger sausage and ribs. All the drinks were free, too, so I decided Buster and I should ditch the body armour like everyone else, and enjoy our meal in the sun. For just a few minutes it was easy to forget where we were and why.

Buster was happy with my choice of food, and happier still that I chose to share it. Still in some kind of false holiday mood I decided to do some shopping and picked up a few gifts in anticipation of my upcoming R&R, which would be just before Christmas. Everyone encouraged me to take Buster into the shops too, and once again he became the centre of attention with the US soldiers who all wanted their photographs taken with him.

We slept well in the section that night, probably because we had had a chance to relax. Buster slumped into a full snoring sleep which I found very comforting. He was lying by my side, stretched almost the full length of my body, one ear scrunched under his head and the other sticking up in the air. I flopped that ear down over his eye and his body sighed a little 'thank you'. He had a couple of dreams, the running kind. Again I hoped he was dreaming about chasing imaginary rabbits in England.

The sleep was good but we had an early start. I gathered our kit and jumped in the wagons and headed for the back gates of Camp Phoenix, where we had arranged to meet our American friends. It was still dark, but some of the locals were going about their business so the now familiar smell of fires and cooking was all around us. I let Buster lead the way with Steve personally covering me with his weapon.

The American soldiers seemed much more cautious. They didn't go too far without the protection of their heavily armoured vehicles, which at the time were much better than ours. It also dawned on me that thirty years in Northern Ireland had made us the experts in this kind of anti-terrorist search work. The American soldiers were openly pleased and relieved that Buster was there.

When we arrived at the compound, the soldiers were forming a semi-queue to stroke Buster and say hello. It was pretty surreal but I was pleased Buster was making such an impact even though it put extra pressure on me to do a good job. I now felt I would be letting Buster and his new friends down if I messed up. As soon as Buster had satisfied his welcoming committee, we started the search – only to have to rethink it almost immediately.

The Americans were very much on edge, and more than once I came round a corner to stare down the barrel of a rifle. It wasn't possible to work under those conditions, so Steve persuaded the Americans to go and secure the perimeter while we carried out the search. Initially they weren't happy to leave us to do the entire search without their brand of intense cover, but Buster was the deciding factor – we knew how he worked best and they didn't.

Buster put in some good work and the area was cleared. There would be plenty of time for the Americans to set up their MEDCAP project, but we had to get back from the compound to Camp Phoenix and the sentries in the watchtowers had reported some suspicious activity around part of our return route. The sensible option might have been to go a different way, but that would have taken us through a number of heavily populated areas which held totally unknown dangers.

Once again Buster was the deciding factor. If the Taliban had taken the time and opportunity to lay IEDs along our path, then Buster would locate them. The decision was taken that he would search back to the back gates of the camp. I wasn't totally happy with this, but that's what he and I do, we search, and this was really no different to any of the hundreds of searches that we had already completed.

Fearing that Buster could be a walking, sniffing target for Taliban snipers, our American friends put up a helicopter as top cover. It flew extremely low over the area, which was brave in itself as the threat of RPGs was extremely high. Seeing that they were prepared to risk a helicopter and pilot for us spurred me on. If they could take that risk, then so should we.

I had been looking forward to my promised R&R but somehow my mind had detached my own need for a break from the realisation that if I was going home Buster would be staying behind. Another handler was being deployed from Camp Bastion to cover for me and look after Buster for the short time I would be away. I thought I didn't mind that, after all I had been through all this before with other dogs. But not with Buster. I had been putting off explaining my going away to the hairy fella but with only hours to go before I was due to pick up a Hercules to Bastion I knew I had to bite the bullet and tell him.

I had already visited his friends Paula and Bobbie to tell them to watch out for him and not to overdo the treats (my latter words fell on well-meaning deaf ears, I'm sure) and the lads were aware that I was going and to expect a new guy – but they were just pleased that Buster was staying. So it was only Buster that I had left in the dark. I chose a mealtime, as I could tell him and then give him his food, which always cheered him up. Having gathered my strength and my words, I walked slowly towards the kennels.

I was usually met by his raucous welcome but this time he had that stoic expression on his face like a loved one who knows they are not going to like what you have to say. I felt instantly guilty.

'Buster don't give me those spaniel eyes, you soft git, I'll be back in no time.' I ruffled his ears as I spoke to him. 'You get a break too, now. Remember the new guy will feed and exercise you, so don't play tricks on him. You hear me? Oh and don't get too bloody fat! Nobody loves a lardy boy!' That bloody dog understood everything I said and it hurt me to leave him. I put his food bowl down as I walked away but he didn't touch it. I turned and waved once more and he was still standing there looking at me. I had to go.

The plan was for me to go to Bastion to pick up the kitbag full of stuff that I really didn't need and then fly to Kandahar to pick up a flight to the UK. After three days of flights to Camp Bastion being cancelled, my plans were falling to pieces. I decided my best hope was to get straight to KIA and sort something, anything out from there.

This is where being in the RAF can have its advantages. I approached the flight sergeant mover and asked him if I could be squeezed onto the next Hercules due out to Kandahar and then – and this was the big one – catch the TriStar flight later that day from Kandahar to Brize Norton. In some bizarre way that would get me home a day early.

He made some phone calls and said that if I got to Kandahar in time then I could get on the TriStar.

True to their word the aircrew and movers worked miracles and turned the Hercules around in double-quick time. When we landed at Kandahar there was a Land Rover waiting there. They quickly took our bags off and loaded us then raced down the taxiway and got us to the plane home.

We were bundled aboard and I'm sure the aircraft was moving as I was taking my seat. It had been a long day and although the TriStar is not the most comfortable of aircraft I was soon asleep.

We landed at Brize Norton bright and early the next day and, unlike most on the aircraft, I found Oxfordshire quite warm compared to Kabul. My brother lives about thirty minutes from Brize, so I gave him a call. I managed to reach him on his mobile only to discover that he was visiting our parents in Oldham, three-and-a-half hours away. If only I'd told him I was arriving a day early! My cunning plan had backfired, and I ended up biding my time in the arrivals terminal at Brize.

Good job I have a great family because when Richie and his wife Katy did arrive I gave them their first problem – I didn't have any clothes. As I never made it to Bastion I didn't get to pick up the kitbag. I'm usually a few pounds heavier than my brother, but since being in Afghan I had lost a good two stone and was able to borrow something from Richie's wardrobe until I could get to the shops.

*

It was coming up to Christmas so the town was packed. I felt very uncomfortable with all the people around me and the noise of the traffic. I wanted to reach for my body armour and my weapon. I looked quickly around for cover from my mates, and where was Buster? I think I even said 'Buster' out loud, but I hope I just said it to myself. I can't be sure. I quickly bought what I needed for the week and got out of there. It was very strange to feel so uncomfortable in my own country.

I went back to Richie's for a second night and was really looking forward to settling in with a few beers and a catch-up. I thought I could handle my drink, but after just a couple I was feeling the effects so I suggested we link up the TV to my camera and have a look at some of my photos from Afghan. I watched my friends from the MERCIAN regiment appear on the screen, and I was reminded just how young most of them were. The thousand yard stare was fixed on most of the faces and for the first time I saw it in myself too. I think even Buster had that faraway look in some of the photos. Katy's parents were round and everyone was very impressed and liked hearing my stories, but it dawned on me just how little understanding the average person has of what we do and go through out there.

Later Richie put on some programmes that he had recorded for me, including the Ross Kemp series and the series about the Royal Marines in Afghanistan. I was later to meet Ross Kemp at an awards event and took the opportunity to thank him for what he had done. He was taken aback and told me not to be stupid, but it is the likes of him and other reporters that help the general public to understand a little bit of the conditions that we face over there. I also explained that the last thing I'd wanted to see on my R&R was a programme about Afghanistan!

As my tour was only six months I was entitled to only a week's R&R. Tracy of course was in Iraq, so I split my time between being at my brother's, visiting my friends at Waddo for a few beers and a catch-up, and visiting my parents and my sister Ali in Oldham. For all of them my weight loss was the main talking point, which made me wonder if I was a real tubs before I left. When I'd knocked on my mother's door, Ali was with her, so I guessed they were tipped off that I was making a 'surprise' visit. There were lots of hugs and tears and questions about Buster and a genuine need to feed me!

You spend all of your tour discussing what home-cooked delights you are going to eat on R&R but when it comes to it, you just don't want to eat. I'm sure that my mum was concerned. I visited my dad and had a few beers and I tried to do some more shopping, but again I couldn't stand the claustrophobia. Oldham has a very large Asian community and while I know the majority are hard-working, friendly people, I found myself eyeing each individual with suspicion and soon had to leave. After months of battling with the ways of a different culture and their beliefs, I felt

I was losing some perspective on real life. War is not a normal way of living, but it becomes normal while you are there and so home becomes the foreign land.

It was strange and before I knew it, it was time to go back. I'm glad I'd remembered to post my Christmas cards first. I'd had some cards printed up with a picture of me and Buster in all our desert combats, body armour and weapons and put it on a Christmas background with the title 'Seasons Greetings from Afghanistan'. I'd wanted to post them in the UK to make sure everyone had theirs in time. One of my corporals from Waddington, Tina, emailed me later to say that she had just received the best Christmas card ever! That was to be a real morale booster.

I didn't feel good about going back but I desperately wanted to see Buster and get back to the job I loved. The time off had given me space to think of what I had been through and how lucky I had been, so far, to survive so much unscathed. These thoughts ran through my mind as I picked up the hire car from Waddo and headed back to my brother's for the night. The check-in times at Brize are ridiculously early so before I knew it was heading back to Afghanistan.

When we landed at Kandahar I discovered that our onward flight was delayed and we would have to spend the night and resume the journey in the morning. As luck would have it, I met up with some Royal Marines that had been with the Vikings and it gave me a chance to catch up and tell them all about

Buster's latest successes. Some of the lads looked terrible – unshaven, ripped combats, even what looked liked blood on their clothing.

We made our way to an area called the 'Boardwalk', which is an area with takeaways, a Green Beans coffee shop and various eateries. The first thing I noticed was that everyone was immaculately dressed and clean shaven. Not the look of the typical squaddie that we were used to seeing. As we walked through I could feel eyes on us and hear the tuts aimed at the lads' unkempt appearance. I can tell you it took a lot to keep my mouth shut and my hands off those men. From that day forward I have carried a dislike for the place and the people there.

When I finally made it back to Souter I dropped my bags and ran to the kennels. I don't know who was happiest to see the other. Buster went into rapture and leaped up to give me a big fat kiss. 'Ah so you haven't forgotten me then? Good, because I've really missed you, you daft dog. Come here!' We had a bit of a wrestle and a few quiet words while I checked that I was still his mate after my week away. The other guy hadn't worked Buster, so they would have only shared the time for feeding and exercise, which meant there was little time for bonding. But I still needed to know and feel that he was *my* dog.

I needn't have worried. He was over the moon to see me and I knew that he would be way more than that when he saw the treats that I had brought back for him. He would have been even more delighted if he knew what was in my bag. The vast amount of Christmas presents for Buster from friends, family and the dog handlers at Waddo was completely over the top! There were tasty gifts for our patrol dogs Bony and Zeus too, but I would leave that distribution job to their handler back at Bastion. I valued my fingers far too much.

I checked in with Bastion to let them know that I was back and raring to go, and was told to get packed up and ready to go on an upcoming operation. It was easy to guess what this would be, as the news had been full of reports from the town of Musa Qala, which the Brits wanted to take back from the insurgents. In a bloodless coup in 2006, the British military had been escorted out by the Taliban, and now we wanted the roles reversed. In an attempt to achieve this aim without too much fighting the Brits' plan had been announced in all forms of media in the hope that the Taliban would just walk away.

The deployment meant leaving Souter, so after packing my stuff and gathering Buster's together we made our rounds of the camp. There were tears and hugs – for Buster – and I was handed several more Christmas presents for him. It seemed strange to have festive wrapping paper in among all of our military kit, especially when we had no idea where we would be at Christmas. Paula and Bobbie were extremely sad to see him go and there were some extra-long hugs for Buster. I knew that he would miss his special 'Kabul cupboard'. Goodbyes said, we climbed into the Saxon and I made my way back to KIA again, with Buster sitting on my lap.

Kabul had been an interesting part of the tour. It was not as action-packed and stress-laced as the Green Zone, but it was filled with its own dangers. I was glad I'd done it and had really enjoyed working with the Coldstream Guards. I always feel a tinge of pride when I watch them on Trooping the Colour now, because we had been made to feel part of them.

That said, I was happy to be going back to the actual war – as strange as that may seem.

CHAPTER 13

Stuck in the Mud

At the airport I met up with another RAF Policeman called Mick Pickering. I knew Mick from Waddington and he was there doing Air Transport Security. Basically it's the RAF version of airport security and customs rolled into one. I joked to Mick that I found it a bit strange that I was carrying my rifle, several hundred rounds, my bayonet and grenades and he was worrying about tweezers in my bag.

We boarded the Hercules and once again Buster was the star of the flight, introducing himself to everyone on-board. As he weaved his magic between the rest of the passengers, stopping along the way to give an extra bit of comfort, sniff a pocket or a bag and generally entertain. Once again I could see just how much people were missing their pets at home and what a quick morale boost Buster could be. He always made everyone smile.

The deadline for the attack on Musa Qala grew closer and Buster and I were to be attached to the Royal Marines who were itching for a fight. Every effort, it seemed, was being concentrated on this operation, everyone's tasks geared around it. There was a constant level of tension and pressure that, in the end … came to nothing. The battle never happened. The deadline came and the first lot of troops just walked in and discovered that the media coverage had done the trick and the Taliban had packed up and left in the middle of the night. Only a group of bewildered locals were there to greet the Forces. This was a huge anti-climax for the soldiers, but in reality it was also a massive victory. A major strategic town had been taken without a shot being fired and, most importantly, without injury or loss of life.

I returned to Bastion for a couple of days' downtime. The weather had definitely taken a turn for the worse. Now the rain had turned the sand into a coarse, sticky mud that everyone was wearing to a lesser or greater degree. I caught up with Mike and Phil and their patrol dogs Bony and Zeus. Mike and Phil weren't having a great time as they had been pretty much confined to Bastion. Mike had been down to Lashkar Gah, but Bony had made such a nuisance of himself that half the locals had stopped coming into work! Consequently, Mike's over-keen patrol dog was brought back to Bastion with his tail between his legs.

Not long after chatting to Mike, I was told that my next stop would be Lashkar Gah and that didn't make me happy. If the rumours were correct, having Buster sit in the section and checking the odd vehicle at the gate was not the best use of his skills – or mine for that matter. I spoke the OC who told me that only private and lance corporal dog handlers had been down there so far and he wanted me, a sergeant, to go down to sort it out. I still wasn't happy as there were some great stories coming out of Sangin and other Upper Gereshk locations. I didn't want Buster to be bored and thought it a waste of a great search dog. It seemed unfair.

Unfair maybe, but it was an order.

An American Blackhawk helicopter took us out there the next morning. Buster headed straight for a window seat. A number of Special Forces personnel were also on-board and the one sitting nearest to the window soon had a spaniel on his knee. Everyone was in stitches and Buster duly obliged when requests flooded in from everyone on-board wanting their photograph taken with him.

The helicopter showcased the landscape down below spectacularly as we followed the Helmand River along its twisting course. There was far more greenery around now the winter had arrived, but the compounds dotted here and there on the outskirts of Lash still attracted the eye. It had become second nature to check them out and only trust what you find, not purely what you see.

'Millionaire Row' is the name given to the string of unexpected and spectacular houses along the riverbank. These houses belong to the government officials. Surrounding them were a lot less salubrious dwellings, a stark reminder that this was a country of the very rich and the very poor.

We landed at Lash, which seemed to be stuck in the middle of a quite well-populated area, and as always there was a quick turnaround. The camp had looked small from the air, but in reality it was even smaller. I made my way to the Dog Section to see what it had to offer Buster. He didn't look in a hurry to get to his bed, probably because he had been power napping on the lap of the Special Forces guy the entire flight, but I always checked the kennels as a priority. The section was similar to FOB Price: a kennel block, an ISO container which doubled as an office and storeroom, and a small seating area. One feature that was missing was running water, due to an ongoing problem with a stand pipe and hose outside the compound. That would be interesting.

And my bed? Well my accommodation wasn't ready, so it was the transit tent for me – a tent with just a few camp beds in it – although I did have the luxury of porcelain loos to look forward to. That night was to be one of the coldest I'd known for a long time. I slept fully clothed in my sleeping bag and wished Buster had been there to be my canine hot water bottle.

The cold night made it a dismal introduction to our new home, so I was eager to take Buster for a walk and then take him to meet some new friends that morning. Of course my dog was up for this. As we walked across the front of the helipad, he darted into a hardened area and immediately indicated on a tin. It turned out that the tin contained flares for the helicopters, so technically he had found explosives which demanded the usual reward – playtime with his ball.

Of course he then tried this trick every time we walked past the helipad. A young South African from 16 Air Assault, who told me what was in Buster's 'find', went by the very unflattering nickname of Maggot, possibly due to her short stature. Her real name was Yolanda, and this petite blonde soldier became one of Buster's biggest fans over the next month.

I made my way to the headquarters; I introduced myself and discussed the best way to use me and Buster as the vehicle checks were a waste of our talents. Fortunately, a detachment of Coldstream Guards would provide the focus for most of our time there. I felt so pleased that I had said something and headed over to the kennels to get Buster. The Main Entrance Point was close to the Dog Section so we walked around the corner. Secure in the knowledge we *would* be getting out on patrol with the Guards, and to keep Buster busy and alert, I offered to carry out a few vehicle searches.

Buster gave me such a filthy look. I felt a bit guilty for not being able to find him something more challenging to do but I was working on that. The Guard Force was made up mainly of 2 YORKS personnel, but supplemented with anybody else that was available. The majority of Lash was made up of officers, so the juniors always got the short end of the stick. But they were all the same to Buster and he made it his mission, rank no problem, to gain as many new friends as possible.

After we'd searched the vehicles I found some space where we could do a little training. This broke the monotony of the vehicle searches and gave Buster some good exercise. The aromas from the mess tent had me thinking about food from very early on, and at lunchtime I discovered it tasted as good as it smelled and was a credit to the chefs. (On one occasion we had lobster. I don't know where on earth they got that from but I wasn't about to pass up the opportunity to give it a try.)

The head chef, a TA soldier, asked if he could come and meet Buster and I told him to come round after his shift when I knew Buster and I would be having a rest. He arrived with a paper bag in his hand and from Buster's reaction it wasn't hard to guess what was in it. Buster sat and put his paw in the air waiting, expectantly. The bag contained a large portion of roast beef, and that day my dog ate better than most Afghanis. Needless to say, our chef became one of Buster's favourite visitors.

Lash was a strange place for us and after our experiences in Helmand, I felt we needed to get out and about, so I approached the OC of the Guards directly and requested that I assist them on patrol and to my relief the offer was accepted. We had a day to prepare for a four-day patrol in Nawa, a town to the South. It's an area surrounded by desert that's well known as a 'pass through' for the Taliban. It sounded as if there would be a job for Buster and we were ready to make the move.

I was up bright and early the next morning and took Buster for a walk around the camp. The only other people up and about at this time were the sentries in the towers. Buster went up to say hello to each one, so our little walk took longer than anticipated. There wasn't much scoff on offer but the guys were cold and Buster was happy to share a bit of warmth with them. The weather was vile and the rain was making the grey mud situation worse. Good job I had dry bags in my Bergan, which protected everything when it was all loaded into the vehicles – four Snatches and four WIMKs (Weapons Installation Mounted Kit – a heavily armoured, but open-topped, Land Rover). Despite the aggressive-looking vehicles this was essentially a 'hearts and minds' operation, so in addition to the patrol members we also had someone from the Military Stabilisation Support Team (MSST) to liaise with the local communities to find out what they needed most – schools, play areas, wells, etc. Dave, a soldier from the YORKS regiment, was also with us. That put three people and Buster in the back of our Snatch.

Due to the filthy weather we took turns at top cover as we headed out of the city towards the bridge over the Helmand River and on to the desert. The journey took us along the sides of canals, and the risk of the road collapsing and us falling in was all too real. I'd been desperate to do some top cover before, but I now realised it was better to be inside the Snatch, as at least you couldn't see the danger approaching.

As we entered the town of Nawa we were stopped by a policeman. Well that's what he said he was, but to me he looked like a fourteen-year-old wearing his dad's old uniform. I got out with Buster to see what all the fuss was about and one look at my dog and the lad ran off to hide, much to the amusement of everyone watching. Buster looked at me as if to say: 'What's his problem? Can we get on with the job now?'

As Buster started searching I could see the lad watching from the doorway and he was clearly fascinated. Eventually his curiosity got the better of him and he emerged from his hiding place.

The town was very busy with a number of shops, but they were all very run-down. Everywhere you looked there was a building that needed repairing. I don't know how many patrols had been through before us, but all the townspeople stopped what they were doing and stared. They weren't hostile but they weren't welcoming either, which was quite unnerving. Buster was searching ahead, his nose working overtime, the mud splattering his coat as he trotted along. He was totally oblivious to everything. I don't know if the locals knew what he was there for or not but once they noticed him they couldn't take their eyes off him.

Buster's nose took us safely into the town where the main street was split by what had probably been a canal but was now a stagnant, green pond. Then I saw something that made me laugh; just to the side of the would-be canal was a flaking painted sign which professed to be from the Ministry for Health. They would have been hard pushed to find a less healthy spot. As we reached the other end of the town we noticed the town's second police station, which was manned by the same ragtag bunch of individuals we met when we arrived. Our young hideaway policeman must have followed us, as he was so impressed with Buster that he wanted to give him a dog biscuit. Normally I would have said 'no' as Buster was on duty, but in the spirit of 'hearts and minds' I allowed it and handed him one to give the dog – only to see the boy devour the biscuit himself. Buster, who had been sitting at my feet shuffling into his regal pose ready to accept the offering, was not amused.

Buster was padding about and looking at me wondering: 'What happened to the biscuit then? Is there another one? I really liked the look of that biscuit!' I told him to stop moaning as he had enough recently to go without a biscuit or two, and we mounted back up into the vehicles to leave the town.

The next village was a short distance away and one thing is for sure, the approach road was not made with military vehicles in mind. As the road narrowed we soon got wedged between a compound wall and a canal. The top cover lads had a good view of what was going on ahead and it wasn't good news. He announced, 'It's total gridlock!'

I popped my head up and saw that we were stuck behind two donkeys that appeared to be in no rush at all. When the traffic eventually filtered through we entered the village and I took Buster on a search while the MSST spoke to the village elder about what we could do to help. Top of his wish list was to have the canal running again, but when we offered to provide the shovels he was less than enthusiastic. He basically wanted us to do the work. I must have been wearing a look of disgust and disappointment as I couldn't see any of the villagers looking busy, but I was away to search more of the village.

Our village-to-village tour became easier once the rain stopped and, although it was cold and overcast, the journey into the desert following the line of the river was less stressful than any other patrol I had been on before. But I couldn't help looking for signs of trouble. A Bedouin camp on the riverbank came into view like a desert mirage. It was suddenly there in our path and although it didn't have the silken splendour of a scene from the *Arabian Nights* it was quite a sight, especially for Buster.

'Hey Buster, look what's here. Remember these?'

Camels are not just the ships of the desert, they are transport and a sign of wealth – and this guy looked as if he had the equivalent of maybe a couple of BMWs back home. We'd stopped and I called Buster out of the back of the Snatch so he could take a closer look. After all, the last time he saw camels it was at dawn and at a distance so now he could get fully acquainted. He approached with caution, to say the least, and if a dog's sense of smell is really 1,000 times more sensitive than a human's then they were going to smell really bad to him. There was a lot of sniffing from both parties and I sensed that the camel owner was getting a bit edgy. He wasn't overly happy with Buster getting so close to his property, so I called Buster off before I had a bill for camel repairs.

Buster could have easily stayed with his new four-legged friends as they weren't bothered about him, but it was time to move on. Buster said his fond farewells and so did we. We carried on into nowhere for a while before coming to a spot where the river was narrow and looked fairly shallow. I was in the front wagon which drove through and up the bank on the other side. We stopped to give cover and had to fire a few flares at local cars that were coming close. It was a popular crossing point so we had to keep our wits about us. As I looked back I saw that two of the WIMKs and two Snatches had got stuck in the sludge of the river. The Land Rover is usually at home in these conditions, but with the added armour and weaponry on-board it was just too heavy.

The two free WIMKs took up defensive positions on the other side of the river while the other Snatch was used to try and pull the other vehicles out. That left just our Snatch on the right side of the river. We were now causing a real traffic jam and a few of the locals tried to queue jump, which meant we had to fire a few flares to keep them at a safe distance. As darkness fell, the drizzle started, and we were going nowhere. We were now sitting ducks.

Dark grey cloud moved in on everything and I could hear the revs of the Snatch as it struggled to pull the other vehicles free. It had to budge. It just had to budge because if we sat there any longer we were going to fall under attack. We had to get out of there as fast as possible and the Snatch was the only way it was going to happen. We took as much as we could out of the trapped vehicles to lighten them, but at the end of the day an armoured vehicle is still about five tons of solid metal.

We called the Snatch the workhorse, and that's exactly what it was for us that night. Those who prayed, prayed; and for those who cursed instead there were shouts of, 'Shift your arse you pile of shit,' and, 'Come on you bloody thing or you'll be razor blades for sure if you don't get us out of here!' Suddenly the Snatch jolted forwards, towing wagon with it. Once that one was safely on the banks the Snatch was back to rescue another out of the water. Eventually there was only one WIMK still stuck fast.

We pulled back to form a smaller defensive circle which made the local traffic take a wide arc around us. In the distance we could see torch lights and car headlights flashing. Word had obviously got out that we were stranded and quite an easy target. I can still remember the creeping terror that took over as soon as we realised that the terrible weather conditions made rescue by a Chinook impossible. If we couldn't shift the vehicle we were going to have to deny it (burning it with red phosphorous grenades) so it couldn't fall into the wrong hands. A WIMK would have been quite a prize for the Taliban.

And if that wasn't enough there was one more problem – our Snatch was still the only vehicle on our side of the river. We needed to drive it back over to join the others.

I'm so glad I wasn't our driver. There was some trepidation – I'm sure everyone's heart was in their throat, I know mine was. All the toing and froing was making Buster restless. I could see him pacing around and always checking in with me, probably hoping I would come up with some answers. Maybe some of my nervousness rubbed off on him. Thankfully due to skill and a helping of luck the driver got us safely over. There was a huge sigh of relief from everyone as we again took up defensive positions. We weren't out of danger yet.

The lights were still flashing in the distance and, to add to our misery, it started to rain again. Just as all seemed hopeless a local truck appeared. One of the WIMKs drove up to intercept it and did a deal with the driver to pull the stranded wagon out with a towing chain. After some very impressive driving, the WIMK was finally dragged clear. After thanks and some American dollars were exchanged, the truck went on its way.

We now had another problem – the WIMK wouldn't start. The underneath was covered in mud. We radioed Lash for assistance only to be told that a rescue would be impossible until the morning, which meant we needed somewhere to spend the night.

I was glad I'd brought plenty of supplies for Buster. He was tired, like the rest of us, and we still had to find a compound prepared to take us in. As we chained the stranded WIMK to a Snatch we could still see the lights in the distance. We were still being watched.

It's a big ask of any compound owner to take a convoy of our military vehicles in, even for one night, but we managed to convince one man it was a good idea – once again the American dollar worked a charm. We drove in and secured the gates. Guards were put on both entrances and the rest of us lit our Hexi stoves and got some much-needed hot food and drink down us. It's amazing how good boil-in-a-bag can taste sometimes.

Buster was as hungry as the rest of us. He had been so patient and mucked in with everyone. I was really proud of him. He enjoyed his tea and then did the rounds in the hope of more being offered up. He didn't mind just licking the pouches out, he was happy for anything and the lads were happy to see him. He was always a great distraction and comfort at times like this. It would have been easy for me to keep him to myself, but I never thought of Buster in that way. He was my dog, but everyone's friend.

A roster was produced for guard duty for overnight and then we got our heads down. There is not much room in the back of a Snatch at any time, but with three people, all our kit and Buster, sleep was going to be a luxury. Also it was freezing cold and we were all still wet after being out for hours and hours manoeuvring the vehicles.

I was glad to have the warmth of Buster on my legs and I think he was glad to have some warmth from me. I certainly had the best blanket that night, but I still slept with one eye open.

Buster, on the other hand, was the only one to sink

so far into sleep that he snored. His heaving, snoring weight was a big comfort, and a constant and welcome reminder that he was with me.

At three in the morning we got the knock to go on watch. To be honest, I was glad to get out of the Snatch and stretch out. Dave joined Buster and me on duty at the back gate where someone had thoughtfully erected a temporary shelter using a bivvy sheet. I heard a noise from behind and realised that the lads from the WIMK had erected shelters at the side of the vehicle, which was the best they could do as there is no cover on a WIMK. They must have been freezing, but at least they could stretch out. It turned out that the noise I had heard was from one of the blokes waking up to find Buster using him as a mattress. I think he was glad of the warmth and didn't try and move him. Buster was soon snoring away again, quite content.

We made a mug of tea and took comfort from the sweet, hot liquid as we made small talk about all kinds of things just to try and stay awake. The stag seemed to drag for hours and there wasn't even a warm bed to look forward to at the end of it.

Suddenly Buster sprang off his human mattress and dashed to the back gate, put his nose against it and barked. We pulled our rifles up and the lads from the WIMK jumped up behind the machine guns. We heard footsteps and then … nothing.

I didn't know my heart could beat that hard. We had been watched all day and it was inevitable the

Taliban would know where we had ended up. The one thing they would also know from observing every move we made that day was how much weaponry we had with us.

To this day I don't know who was there, but Buster's barking may well have just saved us from a battle.

That was enough drama for one night. It was time for an early breakfast – much to Buster's pleasure. Everyone was up putting pots on the Hexi and packing their kit away. The recovery wagon was set to meet us in a couple of hours, but we still had to tow the broken vehicle to a more accessible point. Buster was doing his usual breakfast round and being a general nuisance, begging anything he could. Very embarrassing, but everyone was used to it and didn't mind one bit. He had done more than his job and been a comfort blanket at the same time.

The compound owner's son had come out to watch Buster doing his thing. He was fascinated and sat stroking him for ages. He asked through the interpreter if he could buy him. I told him that Buster would cost the usual $90,000. I'm sure he thought I was serious and said he would ask his father for the money. Maybe his father had enjoyed a bumper year producing opium, but I doubted it as he was grateful for the few more dollars we handed over to the owner for his generous hospitality.

We pulled up at the rendezvous point before the bridge and waited for the big recovery wagon to arrive. We could see the rescue convoy coming from quite a distance and were happy to see them. The wounded WIMK was going to be quite a project for the REME lads to fix and there were quite a few heads shaking as it was hitched up and guns and kit removed. The crew had to be shared between the Snatches, making it even cosier inside. We limped back to Lash where a welcoming committee had gathered to see us back in. It must have been stressful for the guys in the Ops room, knowing that we could have been attacked and there was not a lot they could do about it.

Buster came in for a lot of hugs and I think everyone was relieved to see the rest of us too. After he had finished collecting the adoration, I took Buster to stretch his legs, which, for him, meant dashing over to the helipad and Yolanda. She was so happy to see him and soon had a biscuit on offer. Lash had not been my favourite place but it was certainly a welcome sight that day.

Back at the kennels, I made a cup of coffee and sat on the bench with Buster. I woke up sometime later having dropped off into an exhausted sleep. Buster was still in the same position and still fast asleep.

It had been a long twenty-four hours.

CHAPTER 14

Christmas in the Desert

Before we knew it, it was Christmas Day. To be honest, on a tour it's just the same as any other day really, but with a few extra parcels to open that we had all been saving up. I was up first as always to see to my first duty of the day, Buster. I was always glad to have that first part of the morning just for us and before the 'rush hour'. I opened a few parcels and immediately found that the majority contained presents for Buster. No surprise there. I knew my place.

Then I opened a couple of presents for me and instantly wished that I hadn't. One was from my neighbours back home and was filled with small glittery table decorations that went everywhere. Next I opened one from my brother which contained a sherbet fountain which had split and again went everywhere. My cramped but usually tidy bed space now looked like a sparkly drug dealer's den. I decided to leave the rest for later, gathered up Buster's haul and went to the kennels.

'Merry Christmas Buster!' I shouted, as I saw his little face at the kennel door. He was padding about, smiling and giving it the full works. Did he know it was Christmas? Knowing Buster, he probably did. He must have sensed that the presents I was carrying were for him so I let him unwrap one. I held it and he pulled the paper off. It was a dog chew which he demolished before we set off on our walk around the camp.

It really was Christmas for Buster. As we did the rounds he collected treats and when we reached the mess tent our friendly chef handed me a box containing some turkey 'just for Buster'. We passed the helipad and, of course, Yolanda was there with an extra big box of dog biscuits for him.

Christmas in a Muslim country means that everything carries on as normal, as the local people still trade. For the majority of the camp it was a down day; but not for all of us. The camp needed guarding, food needed to be provided and the helicopters needed to bring passengers and the much-revered mail. Unlike in the UK, no one had a hangover so everyone was present and correct. As well as the normal traffic we had a convoy of supplies coming in so, as Buster and I were on vehicle search duty, we needed to get the larger back gates open to take delivery.

The rain gone, it was quite a sunny day and warm too. Buster and I sat at the back gate on a wooded bench, with Buster getting all the attention from a young female soldier who was on guard. Of course the hairy one soaked it all up. It helped pass the time and make the searches more enjoyable for him. While we were sitting there an officer from Media Ops came over to see if she could take a picture of Buster going about his normal duties on Christmas Day. She wanted to put some tinsel in his collar, which he seemed happy about, although I thought he was more interested in the reindeer antlers she was wearing. It wasn't until I noticed the dog 'selection box' she had under her arm that I realised she had him totally in her power. He would have worn tinsel, antlers and a fairy frock for just one treat from that box. The photo opportunity was a total success with Buster wearing his tinsel and offering a paw for the treat.

When the convoy came in, it was searched, and that was it for our Christmas Day. I took Buster back to the kennel and gave him his turkey, of which he made short work. It is tradition in the British forces for officers and senior NCOs to serve the juniors their Christmas dinner. All the tables had been decorated to make it look Christmassy, but there was a major lack of alcohol. This had one positive: when there's alcohol it normally gets a bit out of hand and the officers and SNCOs end up covered in Christmas dinner. Alcohol or not, everyone seemed to enjoy it and, although I missed home cooking, Buster's chef friend Geoff did us proud.

A week later New Year's Day came and went without much ceremony – and no alcohol. Afghan is not the greatest place to be if you need your New Year alcohol fix. I was OK. Having Buster to care for was a great distraction over there. He needed me and I needed him so it worked fine.

We sat on our bench in the sunshine that New Year's Day.

'Happy New Year Buster! Not much time left for us over here now, mate. Thanks for keeping me safe so far.'

The sun was on our faces and Buster put his head on my lap. We sat there contemplating that it was now 2008. Buster was celebrating having the biggest treat jar ever.

I was celebrating the countdown to going home.

I was sat in the mess having dinner when I spotted an old friend of mine, Si Waite, who had just arrived. It was great to see him and we spent a while catching up. We 'pulled up a sandbag' and exchanged war stories, and I could see that Si was listening to me and thinking he would have similar tales to tell very soon. It was the first time that I had really accepted how much I'd changed physically, as Si at first had thought I was my 'trimmer' brother Richie who had left the RAF eight years before.

Si was with the inaugural RAF Police/Afghan Police mentoring team. Their Force Protection was being provided by members of specialist units. Si said that it would be great to get arms and explosives search dog support for their patrols, and I had no issues with that. I cleared the patrolling with HQ and Lash became interesting again.

Buster was glad to be back in harness and I was happy to be back doing the job, and exorcising the memory of the last patrol when everything could have gone so terribly wrong. Our first patrols took us around the local police stations. Most were dire, dirty places and the amount of syringes lying around was very disturbing. I was concerned about Buster treading on one and couldn't let him anywhere near. To make it worse, human faeces were all over the place and half a dead camel lay in the middle of one compound. The state of the policemen and their equipment was pretty shocking. There was no doubt in our minds that they needed some help and advice and our guys were very up for it.

We searched the police station at Bost Airport, and Buster had only been in the place a few seconds when he indicated on a door. The policeman in charge said that it was their armoury. As work had been slow, I gave Buster his tennis ball as a reward for his 'find'. No sooner had I thrown the ball than all the policemen who were in the mentoring classes poured out to watch my dog chase his ball!

When the Buster show was over, the chief of the station opened their armoury and we were met with a very scary sight. The room was piled high with ammunition, grenades and RPGs, and a good deal of it was rusting and looked very unstable. The lads got straight on to HQ and requested the ammunition technical officers (ATO), the bomb disposal experts, to attend urgently. If this lot went sky-high we were all dead. The secondary problem for us was that we now needed to hang around longer than was safe to be in that one place. Someone notices everything, so there was no doubt that our presence had been clocked and word would have got out regarding what we were up to.

We put out an all-round defence and Buster and I set out on a search to clear a safe way through for the ATO as they drove in. As we moved the defence further out we came across two blown-up police wagons, which were a reminder to all of us just how volatile this place could be. Buster seemed more concentrated than I had ever known him. His nose was working overtime, but his body was at its normal steady pace. In no time we were back at the station having made safe the entire area within our ring of steel.

A few of the Afghan policemen approached us and just stood staring at Buster. I signalled them to come and stroke him, but they kept their distance until eventually the chief stepped forward to do it. It was then a competition as to who would stroke him next. Buster was happy with the attention, but a bit miffed that no treats were forthcoming.

ATO arrived and were not impressed by what they found. They announced that the safest way to deal with such a massive haul was to load it into an armoured wagon, drive it into the desert and blow it up. It seemed like a plan, so the Afghan police loaded the lot as we kept a respectable distance away. The last we saw of it was ATO heading out to the desert while we made our way back to Lash.

We didn't get far before we got a message that a suspected vehicle-borne IED was driving around the area. As usual the vehicle was a white Toyota Corolla – the suicide bombers' vehicle of choice in Afghanistan. We stopped at the bridge over the Helmand River where police were positioned at either end. It was an opportunity to teach them how to do a proper vehicle checkpoint. They were getting the hang of it but then we realised we had another issue. The patrol, and in particular Buster, was attracting lots of local attention.

At one end of the bridge a huge group of children had gathered to watch Buster and one of them was holding a ball. The boy had worked out that Buster was interested in the ball and distracted every time it was tossed up and down. I couldn't blame Buster but I couldn't trust him either. A suicide-borne vehicle was heading in and I needed him to be a full-on search dog. The decision was taken to pull Buster out. The trouble was he had attracted so much attention that there was a crowd there just for him. If the suicide bomber appeared now it could result in more deaths, civilian deaths as well as our own. We had to go.

Working with the Afghan Police was a real education. There was no doubt at all that they had taken to Buster but I'm not sure they understood that he was there to do a job and not entertain. They had plenty to learn and when we joined them on a night patrol of the city we realised we had our work cut out.

We met at the Police HQ, which was quite impressive by Afghan standards, and set off on foot with the Snatches following up. At one stage a vehicle came too close, which would usually result in a flare being fired. But it was these blokes' first venture into the city and the poor local chap was lit up with about ten flares. The rest of us thought it was gunfire and we must have looked a hilarious sight all hitting the deck.

Buster didn't turn a hair and he didn't hit the deck either. He knew flare from gunfire, even if we didn't. His 'look what I'm expected to work with' expression said everything.

Our patrols with Si's unit took us to varying parts of the city, some quite affluent and others extremely poor. Locals were chatted to and generally happy that we were there. Buster was quite happy with his dual role of search dog and 'meet and greet' expert. He looked as if he enjoyed roaming the city and had an air about him almost as if he owned the place. It was quite funny really and very inspiring for some of the lads if they got the jitters about going into some of the poorer areas. Buster just treated it all the same and the people the same. He looked as if he could tackle anything and the lads took their lead from him. There was a lot of 'if Buster can do it we can too'. The lads were very good at keeping the local dogs away from him as well, so that was one thing he didn't have to bother about.

A few hours into one patrol and we received a call that a suspicious vehicle had been spotted in the area. We made our way over there and I naturally pushed Buster ahead so he could do his job, and everyone felt safer seeing him up-front.

As we went forward I clearly missed seeing Buster skipping over a ditch – because when I reached it, I was too late to dodge what turned out to be an open sewer. My right leg sunk deep into it and was covered in all things disgusting. It was horrid, but I was more worried about the scrape on my shin, as the risk of infection would be high. The lads poured a couple of jerry cans of water over it but we decided it was safer to get back to camp. They let me onto the vehicle, but we had to drive with the doors open and my leg hanging out. Even Buster didn't want to know me.

When we got back, Buster gave me a very wide berth while we were unloading the weapons, and followed about ten paces behind me as we made our way to the leaky hosepipe by the kennels. I got as much as I could off me, but Buster still wouldn't come close. When I took off the trousers and put them in a bin bag, he literally turned his nose up at me.

'Buster, you bloody hypocrite. The times I've had to clean fox poo off you and hose you down when you smell like shit, and here I smell of shit and you turn your back. Thanks mate. Thank you very bloody much!'

The only thing that I had to wear was my waterproof trousers, so I put them on, put Buster in his kennel and went to the med centre. Buster was clearly glad to be rid of me – for once he didn't give me the longing gaze as I left.

CHAPTER 15

Who to Trust?

It seemed that Buster was making quite an impression on the powers that be, and a few days later we heard that he (and so we) had been chosen to assist in a joint operation between the Afghan Police and Afghan National Army (ANA). This was going to require a great deal of coordination, not least because, at the time, there was great distrust between the army and police.

The assignment involved a raid on a house which was thought to be the base for a team of suicide bombers. What was really disconcerting was that the raid was going to take place in daylight. I suppose the intelligence had suggested urgency, so the sooner we went in, the better. It would have felt better if we'd had darkness on our side but Buster's nose worked 24/7 and that was the important factor.

When we met the rest of the unit at the gate, Buster and I got into our allotted wagon and we were given our instructions. The plan was for us to set up a cordon with the ANA, the police would move in to make the arrests, and then I would take Buster forward to carry out the initial search. We also had ATO with us to make safe anything Buster located.

The initial stages were textbook strategy. The area was secured with surprising speed and the police went in and arrested four people. It was then our turn.

I went forward and harnessed Buster up. I'm sure he would have sensed, if not seen, my hands shaking. My nerves were massively on edge, knowing that somewhere in this place there was a high probability of hidden explosives and detonators.

I set Buster off on his job. After just a few seconds, I saw his body language change. I knew he had a smell of something. My heart was in my throat as I watched Buster move towards a door at the back of the room. His nose was down and I could see he was starting his little dance and growl. He was so excited I could even see his teeth.

Yet there was no chance to call a 'find' – because in the same moment the police burst into the house and straight through the door where Buster had indicated.

'Fucking hell! Buster, Buster, here, boy!' I called him to me and we ran out of the house as fast as we could.

'What the fuck are you clowns doing? Are you trying to kill us all?' I vented my anger at one of the officers outside, who seemed totally unconcerned.

As if it couldn't get any worse, the policemen then came out in triumph waving the loaded suicide vests around their heads: one of them was actually wearing one. They were all laughing and smiling. While we all dived for cover, the ANA trained their weapons on the triumphant police and it all became a little fraught.

After a short time and lots of shouting, the

policemen eventually put the vests down and ATO took control. Everyone breathed a sigh of relief. We all knew how close we had come to being blown sky high when we were told that two of the vests were armed and ready to use. I was so proud of my dog – and not a little grateful to have come out of such a volatile operation alive.

Once our bomb guys were satisfied, we mounted up with the four prisoners and set off back to Lash. By the time we got there, the helicopter was already on its way to pick up the prisoners to take them to Bastion. We learned that two of them were the handlers and bomb-makers, and the other two were the intended suicide bombers – they were only fourteen or fifteen years old. It was of some comfort that we had just saved their young lives – as well as many others, if the suicide vests had detonated.

While we waited for the helicopter to arrive, I allowed Buster to go and get a biscuit from his favourite person at the helipad. The Chinook arrived and the prisoners were taken away. I still wonder what happened to them. Are they still in jail? Did they decide to change sides? Or have they eventually got to meet their maker?

The next day was a sad one for Buster; Yolanda was leaving to go to Kandahar. She hugged everyone in her section, and then she saw Buster and began to cry. He had affected and touched her so much. With a final biscuit and massive hug, she said goodbye to him and got on to a helicopter. Buster looked a bit confused and then sat and gazed after her until the helicopter had completely disappeared from view.

It was a poignant moment in an already emotionally charged week. I think I was grateful that we were there to say goodbye and wish her well. Just twenty-four hours before, it looked like we wouldn't make it.

Our work with Si's mentoring team took us to the heart of the Afghan community and the real issues that were affecting their daily lives. If we were truly there to help them, then this is what we had to do. On one of our visits, a group of locals told us that they were concerned because some of the local police, who were from a different tribe, had been robbing their compounds. They claimed that the chief of police was the ringleader. We assured them that we would report this on their behalf, which we did on our return to camp.

The next day we were deployed to search at Kandahar Gate – the border between Helmand and Kandahar provinces – and Buster was on top form. I'm not sure if the suicide vest 'find' had geed him up or what, but he was straining at the leash when we reached the search area. To be honest, I wondered if he could already smell something. The area we had to make safe was quite close to the spot where six policemen had been ambushed and hanged by the Taliban over recent days, so everyone was understandably on edge.

I took Buster to one side: 'Calm down now, you have to take this at a sensible pace, OK?' His tongue was out of his mouth and his eyes bulging – this time it wasn't the heat, it was sheer adrenaline. I let him have the leash and away he went, moving like clockwork.

When he had searched the area, I thought I would finish off with the few vehicle searches as it was guaranteed to bring him back down to earth – he hated doing it so much. While Buster was busy I glanced up and noticed several blue lights approaching from the Kandahar direction. Then I realised there were several sets of lights one after another. I asked one of the policemen from our team if he knew what was happening. He told us that it was the chief of police and several units heading to the local ranges. After having just reported the man for stealing we were a bit worried that he was heading in our direction. We were vastly outnumbered and miles from assistance.

Our top cover gunners quietly made their weapons ready and, as the convoy got closer, we realised just how outnumbered we were. We counted at least twenty police and local militia vehicles. As they got closer and closer, gaining speed all the time, we prepared to defend ourselves, not knowing exactly what was going to happen. Then, they just drove straight past us. No one seemed to know where they had come from, what they had been doing or where they were going, but we were all glad that they kept going.

Buster and I only had a few days left in Afghanistan, but there was an opportunity for one last trip out, this time to Garmsir. I couldn't help thinking about our friends the MERCIANs, as this is where they had been based before we met up with them in Gereshk. That all seemed like a distant memory now as a lot had happened since then, most of it I'm sure I had been trying to forget. I think there is a tendency to try to 'forget' the incidents that have played the most on your mind. I'm sure that's down to self-preservation and sometimes it can work. But not always.

Our last trip of the tour was a reminder of how it all started with Buster, bustling in and making his presence felt among new friends. We moved around the sangars – small temporary protective structures – in the FOB and he was fussed by everyone he came into contact with. The way the lads opened their arms to greet Buster showed just how much they missed their dogs back home, and as usual Buster made the best of the situation by helping himself to ration packs and sweets.

I noticed a great piece of typical squaddie's black humour: in one sangar a sign had been erected saying 'Targets Fall When Hit'. This instruction is given on the shooting ranges, but the difference in Afghan is that the targets are real.

The next day I started to pack our things ready for the move out and my journey home. I took my rifle to the REME (Royal Electrical and Medical Engineers) lads who had been sharing my tent, and they kindly sprayed it with compressed air to get rid of all the sand and grit that was hard to get to. Later that day

I took my kit to the helipad and met the Chinook bringing in the new handler, a young RAVC (Royal Army Veterinary Corps) lad, and his dog, who looked so excited at all the new scents he was picking up. I felt sorry that I only had just enough time to show them to the kennels, hand over the instructions for everything, and show him to the accommodation, before it was time to collect Buster and fly out. We did the rounds and said our goodbyes – Buster gratefully receiving all the adoration – before we ran over to the helipad. Then we waited, and waited, and waited.

The weather was closing in and it was getting late. The likelihood of the Chinook coming through was getting very slim so I wasn't surprised when it was confirmed. This was worrying, as we were due to fly back to the UK the following day. If a helicopter didn't come the next morning, then a road move would have to be arranged. This was by far a more dangerous route home. It's a thought that no one relishes, but you can't help it going through your mind at times like this: I didn't want to be killed on the last day of my tour.

I took Buster back to the kennels and then it dawned that I no longer had a bed. So I got my warm kit and spent the night on the section floor with Buster keeping me warm. I woke up, even though I had not really slept, and took Buster for a walk via the helipad. The Chinook was due in an hour. This was to be the start of a journey that would last for a very long fifty-seven hours.

As usual, some of the lads helped me with my kit while I looked after Buster. I didn't have time to register much emotion as we had to jump on quickly and just a short ride later Bastion was below us. 'Well, there it is Buster. The first leg of the journey home, but it's been OK hasn't it? We're OK aren't we? We made some good friends and you've still got most of your treat jar left!'

I think 'treat jar' had become a new bit of Buster's vocab. His ears pricked up when you said it.

As we landed I realised that my dog and I were the only ones getting off, as the rest were off to Musa Qala, so this time I had to carry my own kit as well as keep hold of Buster. Somehow, in the thinking about how I was going to carry everything, I managed to throw on my Bergan, grip my patrol sack and overbalance, smacking my shin on the ramp on the way out. All the way through a tour and now I had managed to damage myself on a helicopter on the way home. Typical.

Mike was there to meet me and shared the news that we wouldn't be flying out until much later, so we had time to waste. We went over to the Dog Section and I was debriefed by the new OC, Major Dick Pope, who thanked me, Mike and Phil for our efforts in Afghanistan and presented us with our NATO medals. Although we can't wear these on our uniform, they are a nice keepsake and it felt good to have our efforts recognised. The mini-ceremony over, we left to prepare the transit kennels for the dogs and bundle our weapons. I put Buster in his kennel for a rest. I thought I was doing the best for him, but he still gave me that withering look that he is so good at.

Darkness came and with it the Hercules which would take us all the way home. Usually you wait outside the Hercules terminal, but this time the movers allowed us into their heated tent. Everyone was happy to see Buster and made a great fuss of him, but patrol dogs Bony and Zeus were given a wide berth. While they were so angry with the world Buster gave them a wide berth too. We boarded the aircraft and settled the dogs into their kennels. Buster and Zeus went quietly, if a little unhappily, but Bony still wanted to inflict pain on anyone that came near him. After all this time he was still struggling to differentiate between friend and foe.

On went the body armour, helmets and ear defenders before we took our seats. The doors started to close and I looked out at our last sight of Afghanistan. I was really happy to be going home but I couldn't help feeling a slight tinge of sadness that the adventure was at an end. I had experienced some great adventures and met some great people, but as the engines revved and we sped down the runway it really was all over. Rising into the darkness I had tears in my eyes – I'm not sure if they were tears of relief or sadness.

The good thing is when you're on an empty aircraft you can stretch out on the floor. I put my roll mat down, put my iPod on and the soothing hum of the engines soon had me fast asleep.

I woke up some time later and went to see how Buster was doing. I could tell he wasn't happy to be there and his back was turned to me, but at least he was curled up on his vetbed and looked quite comfortable. We made our first stop at Al Udeid to let the dogs out for a quick toilet break and a leg stretch. Then we headed for the mess tent, where everyone was dressed in sports gear or normal combat uniform – not a helmet, body armour or a weapon to be seen. We ate on real plates with proper metal cutlery, sitting on proper chairs. I had almost forgotten what that was like.

We were offered cans of pop, packets of crisps and biscuits, and we stuffed our pockets as if we were going to go without food for a week. But to be honest, I kept more than a biscuit or two back for Buster.

Back on board the Hercules, I went to give him a treat in the hope that he would see it as a peace offering. He took it from my very gently, without looking at me, so I don't think I was entirely off the hook. Cyprus was still a long way off so I thought I should take a leaf out of Buster's book and get some sleep.

Hours later we approached Cyprus, which meant quarantine for the dogs and one step closer to home for the handlers. Two old pals from the Dog Section, Jock Muirhead and Lucy Farmer, were there to meet us with a crate of Warsteiner beer. Any beer was likely to knock our heads off after our being dry for so long, but this stuff was lethal. It promised to be a night to remember.

We got the dogs off and the crew told us that we would be here for the next fourteen hours and then UK bound. Mike, Phil and I walked our dogs to the section, each of us going in different directions. This was under the pretence of being able to give the dogs a good run without interference, but really it was so we could say our goodbyes with a degree of dignity.

I took Buster over to a field for a really good run. He automatically checked it for explosives. We sat down and had a big cuddle and Buster licked my face. I couldn't help but wonder what I was going to do without him.

Perhaps he felt the same, because he let out a little whine as he shuffled closer and leant his weight against me.

'Hey, it's going to be alright, my friend. I'll be back in rainy old England and you'll be here in the sun enjoying yourself. Everything will be fine and we will be together again very soon.

'Thank you for keeping me safe, Buster. You're a good dog, you know that? Well, you are.'

I gave his curly coated ears a good ruffle as I spoke to him – and I'm sure he understood every word.

When we got back to the Dog Section I gave Buster his breakfast and left him doing one of his favourite things – eating. Meanwhile, I made a dash for the Dog Section rest room and had a couple of beers. It wasn't long before we were feeling the effects and took up the offer of a full English breakfast in the mess. That, along with another can of beer, was heaven. We were shown to our accommodation, but none of us slept. Instead we wandered around Akrotiri camp, enjoying our freedom and meeting up with more dog handler colleagues, catching up on war stories and updates from the outside world. By the time we had to leave, we were definitely feeling the effects of the beer and were driven back to the aircraft – via the Dog Section. I had to see him once more before I left.

Buster was stood in the middle of his kennel and didn't even come to the front. He knew something was wrong. I went to him and gave him a great big cuddle. All he gave me was a look that broke my heart.

As soon as I left him, I felt very alone. We had shared some rough times during the tour and now it was over there was the usual quarantine period for Buster. I'm sure he needed the rest but I really didn't want to leave him. The next six months were going to be very long and lonely without Buster at my side.

Back on the plane, the beer must have kicked in and the next thing that I remember was waking up on our approach into Lyneham and good old England. We arrived at about 0330 hours. Our connecting transport was late. When the young handler arrived from RAF Waddington he got a tongue-lashing. Some four hours later I was home.

But home without Buster just wasn't right.

CHAPTER 16

Home at Last

The next few months were difficult. I found myself getting angry in crowds and on nights out. I was also having bad dreams and reacting to loud bangs. I know I was missing Buster's calming influence. I don't think I'd fully appreciated this when we were together in Afghan, but without him I was lost.

Shortly after getting back to work, I got a phone call from Sergeant Dave Brooks, a long-time friend of mine who was running the Cyprus Dog Section. He told me that a vehicle search dog had failed its licensing in Afghanistan and that Buster had been sent back there. I was furious, not just because I thought he deserved a break, but also because I knew he hated searching vehicles. I hated the thought of him being back in Helmand so soon, and without me being there for him. I knew the dangers out there and I couldn't do anything to help him. I felt so helpless.

So began the months of wondering what Buster was up to. I wondered if he was behaving himself for his new handler and hoped he wasn't playing him up. Buster could do that if he wanted to. Even before he came to me, Nick had told me he was what some handlers politely call 'full of character'. He knew what he was doing, so it was just the rest of us that needed to watch our step. If he sensed over-confidence he would pull a little stunt to bring the handler back to earth. If the chap was still gaining his confidence, our seasoned war dog could very politely take charge and take them through their paces. You worked *with* Buster, not above or below him. He levelled you off or brought you up to scratch and then brought out the best in you.

After a little while I heard through the grapevine that Buster had been partnered with Si Pound, an old friend of mine, so I knew my dog would be just fine and no doubt get his fair share of the rat packs and treats. I was more worried about Si. I knew he would be enjoying handling Buster because he's fun and you feel safe with him, but I emailed him to warn him that the old dog would be putting him through his paces.

Si later told me that he did indeed experience Buster's fourteen vehicle maximum, and got a bit of a nip when Si tried to prise the hairy one off the seats in the fourteenth vehicle's cab. Buster also developed a new technique of lying behind one of the vehicle's wheels when he'd had enough. Trying to encourage him away from the spot ended in a nipped hand! When Si told me, I could only remind him of what (I had said, 'Told you so!' (I was also rather pleased that Buster had never nipped me.)

In December 2008 I got the news that Buster was on his way home after his tour and the quarantine. The few days leading up to his return seemed to really drag, but when I heard for sure that he had started his journey back to the UK I couldn't wait to leap in the dog van and go and collect him. He was flying into RAF Lyneham and I knew they would want to move him through the system pretty quickly. I just hoped that his pet passport was up to date. His health would be the main concern so all I had to hope for was the all-clear from the DEFRA vet.

I timed it perfectly. I caught a glimpse of Buster in the transit kennel and I'm sure he could smell me, even if he couldn't see me, because his head was swishing quickly from side to side trying to find me. I couldn't wait to open the kennel door. 'Buster! Hey, it's great to see you! What've you been up to?' We had a great reunion with lots of licks from him, and strokes and fuss from me. He looked well, and I told him so. I think he must have been tired but he was bearing up as he always did and I knew he would be OK once he was home in Lincolnshire.

Before we left Lyneham we went for a big walk, not just to stretch Buster's stumpy legs and give him a breeze out, but so we could spend some quality time together. It was great to see him scooting through the grass, sniffing and rooting around in the sweet English earth. He was so tail-waggy happy and it made me feel the same just to watch him. Every now and then he checked in on me: just a quick glance back here and there, and other times he ran to me and dodged and weaved through my legs until I threw his ball again and we had a good old chase. Buster was back in my life and I felt more like me with him at my side. Maybe that was because we had shared so much? I don't know what created the bond but I do know that everything was better when he was around.

It was late when we got back to RAF Waddington and I wondered whether to put him in the kennel block for the first night, but when he threw me the big spaniel eyes I caved in and took him home to meet Tracy. Going there also meant that he would meet our other dogs, Dago and 'Little' Buster, for the first time.

Having two dogs named Buster (and both spaniels) was not the best idea ever, but there was a sentimental reason behind it. Our last two pet dogs, Hobo, a German shepherd, and my retired drugs detection dog Guy, a springer spaniel, had died the previous year. After I returned home from Afghanistan and Tracy from Iraq, Tracy suggested that we gave two dogs a home as soon as possible, as life really was unbearable without dogs. I didn't resist.

We went for the same breeds again and had no trouble finding a name for the German shepherd – Daggo – but the springer spaniel remained nameless for a while, until Tracy had an idea, 'Let's call him Buster after your worker. What do you think?'

At the time I thought it was a brilliant idea, then I would have a Buster at home, although he wasn't quite the same. But the night I brought Buster home from Lyneham I realised that our idea was not so brilliant after all.

I don't think 'Big' Buster was overly enamoured with 'Little' Buster, who decided to be a full-on mischievous little sod who wouldn't leave him alone from the moment we arrived home. But Big Buster was so impressed with the massive collection of dog toys that he decided he wanted them all for himself. He collected them all up, sometimes carrying up to three in his mouth at once, made them into a nest and lay on top of the lot, growling at the other two when they came near. It was hilarious to see him with all the toys in a big heap and Daggo and Little Buster sitting looking forlornly at him.

The next drama was teatime. Buster had always been very precious over his food, wolfing it down before any other dog could get a sniff. Unsurprisingly he was just the same at home but added a bit of a growl to warn off the others, who were actually busy eating their own meals and without the drama. Buster's table manners were going to be a work in progress but we all survived the first night and it was interesting to see Daggo and Little Buster giving the new dog his space to settle in. They worked it out for themselves and just stood and watched him do his thing without interruption. They just accepted him.

CHAPTER 17

The Last to Leave

The huge deployment of service personnel, and dogs, to Afghanistan had overshadowed the work that the dogs and handlers were still doing in Iraq. Arms and explosives search dogs had proved their worth many, many times over there, and way before my Buster's time another spaniel called Buster had been awarded the Animals' VC in 2003 for locating a deadly cache of weapons and bomb-making equipment hidden behind a wardrobe in a home in Safwan, southern Iraq. Without doubt that haul saved many, many military and civilian lives, and the dog had succeeded where an earlier search by humans had failed. When the mass withdrawal of troops began that Buster remained on duty. But it was *my* Buster who was to have the honour of being the last British Military Working Dog to leave Iraq in 2009.

The opportunity for me to return to Iraq came in January that year. I heard there was a detachment coming up and they would be looking for an Ops sergeant. I was keen to go – we all thought it would be the last chance to see service there. I signed up for it knowing that Buster would be going too, and that I would have to watch him being handled by someone else. As Ops sergeant, this tour would be less hands-on for me – more overseeing the dogs do their job. What I needed to do was team Buster with a handler I could trust.

Corporal Terry Sargeant stepped up for the job, and I know Terry won't mind me saying this but it was very difficult watching Buster work with someone else. There were times when I really didn't like it. As I've said, it's like seeing your wife with another bloke – it hurt. But I have to admit there were some amusing moments too. Terry was relatively new to working with arms and explosives dogs, so Buster often gave me the look, 'What *is* he doing?'

We have some excellent training areas in Lincoln and it wasn't long before Terry and Buster were working as a team. Terry was definitely the one learning the most, but Buster was being a real gentleman and I could see the mutual trust building between them.

As is sod's law, just before Buster and I deployed to Iraq, Tracy was sent to Portsmouth on a course. It was great that she could come home every weekend leading up to my departure, but on the last day we had together the emotion all came to a head. We took Big Buster for a long walk and I knew that she was sad at the thought of him going away for what could be another year. Tears flowed. I'm sure she was a bit upset I was going too, but I don't think either of us realised until that moment what a big part of our family Buster had become. Even before he came to live with us I'd told Tracy about him in every letter and every phone call. He was a part of our family. A part of us.

The dangers that our service dogs face are very real. The death in Afghanistan of RAVC dog handler Kenneth Rowe and his bomb dog Sasha, who were killed in action in July 2008, realised the biggest fear that haunts every one of us and our families. Buster had already faced and survived a great many dangers and he was seen as a lucky talisman by many of the lads he served with, from Bosnia to Afghanistan. All Tracy and I wanted now was for his luck to hold out on his final tour.

On the Tuesday following that sombre weekend, Buster and I made our way out to Brize Norton for the next day's flight out to Iraq. Thirteen of us met up and settled our dogs into the Dog Section, booked our baggage into the air terminal and went to the Gateway House, the transit accommodation at Brize, for our last couple of beers.

Buster was very calm that morning – and maybe a bit sad too. He was a mate and I needed to make sure, as far as I could, that he was OK. We had a chat before we left the section and I explained to him that I would be with him but Terry would be his handler, and once again I saw that knowing look that to me said he understood. He licked my hand as I stroked his muzzle. 'Good lad, Buster.'

I called my brother Richie to arrange for him to come over, but I got a lovely surprise when Tracy answered the phone. She had hired a car to come up from Portsmouth to say goodbye. I can't deny there was a tear in my eye. It gets you like that sometimes, especially when you're trying to hold it back. I'm not sure what Buster made of that but I do know that he enjoyed the walk in the cool of the evening and feeling the smoothness of the grass under his mossy feet. He had no idea that he was just a walk away from setting his paws down in the sandy place.

At 0500 the next morning we were up to exercise the dogs and get them over to the aircraft pan. We were flying out on the same C-17 that took us to Afghanistan, and I always think of it now as our personal plane. An hour-and-a-half later we landed at Hanover for a two hour stopover before going on to Incirlik in Turkey, then Kuwait. It was there we boarded the Hercules for Iraq and for the first time since we left home shores we had to don body armour and helmets for the landing into Basra.

Rocket attacks were still a daily occurrence, so the movers were keen to hustle us off and through to hard cover. As we stepped off the plane, we were hit by the unmistakable smell of the Middle East: dusty, sweet and oily. Nowhere else I've been smells like that. The briefing started immediately along with the lectures and warnings on 'what to do in the event of an attack', and then we were bussed to the terminal. Bags and weapons on board, our welcoming committee, the outgoing handlers from the RAVC, helped us load the dogs on the trucks bound for the Dog Section. We were going to have a week for the handover and the place was going to be pretty crowded till the Vet Corps left.

The kennels systems that were used were professionally converted ISO containers that were self-contained and had a kennel area, a free run, and storage for food and water. It was a little bit of luxury for the dogs, who enjoyed the benefits of heating or air-conditioning to suit. In contrast, our accommodation was not so luxurious: twenty-man tents fitted with 'coffin beds'. A coffin bed is about as grim as it sounds – a cot bed surrounded by breeze blocks and with a steel roof topped off with sandbags. Not great for the claustrophobics among us for sure, but they did have a massive advantage – if the attack alarm went off in your sleep, you could just stay put instead of running for cover.

It was at this point that the media entered our lives. We already knew that Buster was a special dog but now the rest of the world had cottoned on to the incredible fact that this was Buster's fifth major operational tour of his career. I was talking to the press and Buster was giving them all his usual military poses for the cameras. Buster's face was all over the national British press and he made it to the front page of my local paper in Oldham. My family was so proud of him.

I was lucky that Terry didn't mind all the fuss despite there being a job to be done. The thing was, everyone knew that Buster deserved the attention. A dog who has completed more tours than many human service personnel is pretty special and there was a great deal of respect for him. Also, I think people loved hearing about him because he's a dog you can relate to. If he had been a human all the lads would have enjoyed a pint with him. He was that kind of dog.

While the journalists gathered to cover war dog Buster's story they could see how important the dogs were to the operation – and the soldiers. While the guard and patrol dogs protected the camp from thieves, Buster was out with Terry clearing a safe path for the nightly convoys, taking all the equipment back to Kuwait for the onward sea trip to the UK. Several routes were devised, and some were more hazardous than others. The Brit dogs were being used at full stretch. At the same time, the British military presence was being reduced and the American increased. Our days were numbered in Iraq and we could feel it happening.

Not wanting to be outdone by the growing US contingent, we organised a fundraiser for Help for Heroes. We kept it simple: we walked the dogs round the Basra camp and, in exchange for a hug and a cuddle with the dogs, people gladly parted with their money. And guess who lapped up the attention? Buster was in hug heaven! It's the kind of event he could have organised himself and make it a total success. Thanks to him and his furry friends we made a lot of money for a cause dear to all our hearts, and managed some great PR for Buster and his mates too.

It was a very intense and busy tour for Buster, and for the handlers too, but there was one major incident that stopped everyone in their tracks and cast a cloud over the entire tour. Our hearts went out to one of our number, Corporal Cliff Cullen, whose dog sadly lost his life in the line of duty.

Cliff and his dog Benji were searching and making safe a bridge, following some information from the local intelligence. The report had indicated that the bridge had been laced with explosives, making it a danger to everyone – military personnel and civilians alike. Benji's job was critical, so many lives now depend on his search skills. Benji was well into his search when he suddenly disappeared. A gasp went up from the patrol, who raced to the point where he had fallen. Cliff and the rest of the team did their best to get him to the field hospital but, despite the best of care, Benji did not survive his injuries. He must have lost his footing as he worked along the structure, and slipped. We had lost one of our own and we were devastated.

The news of Benji's death affected the entire team. For the handlers, a big part of the sadness was 'I'm glad that wasn't my dog'. It was a handler's worst nightmare and Cliff was living it right in front of us. I went to see Buster in the kennels that night and gave him an extra hug – just because I could.

From the moment we arrived in Iraq there was a feeling that we would not be there for the full six-month tour so it was no surprise when, at the three-month stage, we were told to prepare to move out.

By mid-June 2009, the time we were ready, the section had been stripped down with the kennels sent to the UK for forwarding on to Afghanistan. We passed on some of our equipment to the Iraqi Police for their new section and the rest was taken by the American dog handlers who had moved onto our patch.

We made an early morning departure courtesy of a Merlin heavy-lift helicopter and last to load were the homeward-bound dogs, which included patrol dog Bony, Buster's 'friend' from Afghanistan. Bony was all hair and teeth that morning, he never liked the moving around time, so he was muzzled – just in case. The only dogs not on-board were Buster and one of the patrol dogs. We were due to meet up with them in Kuwait in two days' time, after they had worked the last convoy out of Iraq.

The night before we left I'd taken Buster for a long run and we'd had a great time playing and messing about. In a quiet moment before I'd given him his food, I'd explained what was going to happen next. I felt better telling him, although he would find out for himself when I didn't materialise the next morning. 'Stay safe now, Buster, do you hear me?' I said, looking right into his eyes. 'See you in a couple of days – so just you behave and I promise to do the same. OK?' I held his head in my hands and gave his ears a good ruffle, then left him enjoying his food.

The Merlin helicopter lifted off and we watched Basra disappear for the last time. Everyone was pretty subdued until we flew over a known danger zone and the aircrew let off several flares. Bony was quick to react and flew into a frenzy which set the other dogs off too. Luckily the handlers had a good grip on them otherwise there would have been trouble. I couldn't help thinking about Buster and how he would have probably been asleep and not turned a dog hair. He really could be the king of cool.

Once at Kuwait we erected a makeshift kennel area within the Dog Section. It was a fenced off compound with a set of kennels and a building for when the teams escorted the convoys down. As we were going to be here a few days waiting for our Hercules, it made sense to create a safe area for the dogs and, as there wasn't going to be much to do, I rostered a duty handler and made a training regime in order to stop the dogs and handlers from getting bored.

Some of the lads went over to the American Military Working Dog Section where our fallen dog Benji had been laid to rest. The lads wanted to make a proper job of Benji's grave and this downtime seemed a meant-to-be opportunity. We painted stones black and red, the colours of the RAF Police, and made up a headstone. A couple of days later, the padre conducted a funeral service at the graveside, and I can tell you there wasn't a dry eye to be seen – and that included the American handlers who attended. When these things happen what really hits you is the massive mark of respect and love that we all have for our dogs.

One night there, we were woken up by the duty handler. A sandstorm had swept in and the force of it was threatening to collapse the makeshift kennels, so it was all hands on deck to stop the dogs escaping.

Buster had arrived that day and so my first thought was for him. We quickly piled on some clothes, including hats, gloves and mouth coverings, and made our way over there.

It was horrendous. A wall of sand hit us in the face as we stepped out of the tent. We were totally blind and forced to stick to the tent line just to retain our bearings. When we reached the kennels it was just about possible to make out that a number of the tie wraps had snapped and the kennels were only just standing. We took a few of the patrol dogs out so we could work safely on securing the wraps before the whole thing took off.

The dogs were covered in sand and didn't look too impressed. They were pretty much a line-up of sand sculptures, well sand blobs, with just their ears and eyes showing through. Buster looked particularly unimpressed.

'Hey Buster, what've you been up to? Come here, you daft sod. Have you seen yourself? You really are a desert dog now with all that sand to prove it!' I couldn't help laughing at this rather indignant dog sitting bolt upright in a raging sandstorm, looking like some kind of King Canute character, ordering back the tide of orange sand. He was not amused but I thought it was hilarious.

All safe and gathered in, the dogs soon recovered from their sandy experience and were treated to an extra grooming session the next morning. Buster had gained a new nickname while he was over there and it was down to the fact that he needed a damn good haircut. The liver-brown hair on his legs had become so long that he looked as if he was wearing baggy trousers. 'Buster Brown Trousers' suited him very well and what's more he was happy answering to it.

'Haircut, Buster, that's what you need my lad,' I told him straight. 'But it's something we can sort when you're home, you'll have to do as you are for now. Not long to go I promise you.'

Now the deployment was over, I claimed Buster back and we went for some long walks and played with his ball. When he ran to me I opened my arms and filled them with bounding spaniel. Buster looked tired and he was moving a little slower than usual but Buster was still Buster, just a little fatigued. It was great to have him back with me again and I was determined that this would be his last trip away. He had done more than his fair share of duty for Queen and country.

When it was time to make the next part of our journey home we suddenly realised that we had a problem. Everything had been arranged from Iraq and somehow certain details had been lost in translation. The air-conditioned vehicle that we had requested to transport the dogs turned out to be refrigerated! And somehow the fact that our kennels did not collapse was lost too. Our only option was to pile the kennels on the back of a pickup truck and lash them down for the journey to the airport. The pile didn't look too steady but the truck didn't need to hurry. As for the dogs, they had to travel with us on the coach. We got some strange looks as we drove through Kuwait with a dog looking out of every other window.

It was a relief to eventually board the Hercules. We had sat around for a while until the sight of the mighty aircraft came into view and we watched it circling overhead. It meant we were just one more flight away from home. I got a strong feeling of déjà vu as we approached Cyprus and saw the blokes from the Dog Section waiting to collect us from the aircraft pan. Sergeant Dave Brooks was there and told me about the plans for the next two days. I reckoned a trip to the local waterpark and a barbeque would get the Iraqi sand out of our system.

I took Buster for some long walks and plenty of trips to the beach. He was in his element swimming in the warm Mediterranean. But I was aware that every day we spent together was a day closer to me having to return to the UK and Buster working out his quarantine in Cyprus alone. We had done the tearful goodbye thing several times now but it wasn't getting any easier. I approached Dave and made him promise that he wouldn't let anyone send Buster away again.

'So, Buster, here we go again. It's retirement for you, my lad, and the smell of lush green grass and English river water. It's time to hang up your harness, mate. Don't you worry, we'll be together again soon – and this time for good.'

I made him a promise; a promise I knew I was determined to keep.

CHAPTER 18

Buster the Famous War Dog

Due to the lack of flights and heaps of red tape, it was to be nearly ten months before I saw Buster again. I phoned Cyprus on a weekly basis and was assured that he was fine, and it helped to know that one of the kennel maids had taken a shine to him and treated him to frequent trips to the beach.

At long last, I got the call to collect Buster from RAF Lyneham. Tracy had been deployed to Afghanistan and I knew she would be upset to miss his homecoming. This was the call we had both been waiting for and now I would have to meet him on my own.

In March 2010, I drove onto the aircraft pan and the rear ramp of the Hercules dropped down. Another friend of mine, Bart Ripley, had escorted Buster back and I could see that he was in instant panic. He quickly said, 'It wasn't me!'

I didn't know what he was talking about until the kennel door opened. Buster had been clipped and looked very smart but then I saw his head. 'Christ, Bart. What the bloody hell happened here?' For some reason the 'clipper' had decided to leave Buster with what looked like dreadlocks.

'Will, they were going to dye it pink so it could have been worse,' Bart said.

I was glad they had thought better of dying it, but when we got to the section I grabbed the nearest pair of scissors and got rid of the mess. And it was a good job I did, because over the next few months we found ourselves on a mad media merry-go-round.

Buster was a famous war dog, and everyone wanted him on their show and in their paper. I was happy to be his personal valet and chauffeur which, for a little while, was a full-time job! He was wheeled out for every visiting dignitary and was in every RAF publication going. It got to the stage where my colleagues in the Dog Section played the 'Where's Will?' game every time the *RAF News* or *Provost Parade* came out.

At the 2010 RAF Police Dog Trials at RAF Henlow, we were asked to do a demonstration during the interval, which was a great honour. Then Buster collected the Tosh Thomas Memorial Trophy for 'The biggest contribution to the RAF Police Military Working Dogs over the past year'. I was stunned and delighted and very proud of him.

It was great that Buster was there to receive his award 'in person' because even before he came home from Cyprus we were nominated for the *Sun* Military 'Millies' Awards under the Most Outstanding Airman category. Winning through to the final stages, Tracy and I attended the glittering event at the Imperial War Museum, meeting Princes William and Harry, Prime Minister Gordon Brown and a host of stars from film and TV. We lost out to a very brave Chinook pilot, Flight Lieutenant John Walmsley, who saved the lives of several American troops by airlifting them following an explosion. A brave man indeed. I liked the idea that Buster and I were entered as a team for the Most Outstanding Airman title. We were regarded as 'one' entity, a true reflection of everyone regarding him as a mate, a fellow airman. That's how I'd always seen him. The only pity was Buster wasn't there to enjoy the event too.

Tracy came home from Afghanistan in October and it was a great reunion with all three dogs vying for affection. Buster was still collecting the toys and sitting on them so nothing had changed for her on that front. And as if Buster hadn't enjoyed enough notoriety, I was told that we had won the title Military Dog Handling Team of the Year. We all travelled to London for the ceremony and I have to say I swelled with pride when Buster's achievements were read out to the guests. It was an amazing reflection on what we had been through together. And he was very well behaved sitting next to a Metropolitan Police dog who had been injured in the Tottenham riots.

Military working dogs are not routinely awarded medals, but Air Dog Buster was given special permission from the Military Medals Office to wear his five campaign medals. The RAF Police asked him to be their mascot for the rest of his life, which is an absolute honour. The position came with a special ceremonial coat in striking RAFP red and black with the crest on each side. The jacket proved a little too big, so Tracy took it into the tailors at RAF Cranwell to be altered, and when she told them it was for Buster they kindly did the work for free.

When Buster puts on that coat he takes on a military bearing, he looks every inch a war hero. He first wore it when he was guest of honour at the RAF Waddington Air Combat Power Week. It is the RAF event of the year and showcases the capabilities of the service aircraft and the ground trades. The main visitors to the event are staff officers from the UK and other Allied Countries, but the first day is the Press Day, attended by all the national and international media.

Buster and I were put on the Force Protection stand and our tent was dedicated to the RAF Police contribution to Operations. We had several policemen representing the various jobs that we do including camp security, air transport security, biometrics, prisoner processing, police mentoring, weapons intelligence, counter-intelligence, close protection, special investigations and of course dog handling. I felt a bit sorry for my colleagues as the majority of visitors made a beeline for Buster, who was sitting at the entrance resplendent in his ceremonial coat complete with his row of miniature medals. He caught the eye of a photographer from the *Daily Express* and the image that appeared in the paper the next day started a new avalanche of media requests. The phone didn't stop ringing. Everyone wanted Buster.

We were wanted for TV, radio and a myriad of other things. A photographer came to our house the following weekend to take some more photos for a double-page spread. The words and the photos inspired poems and paintings of him proudly wearing his coat and medals. It was at that stage that Buster also started to receive his own fan mail and dog treats from all over the world – it arrived in sacks!

News of Buster's achievements brought home to people that the military working dogs were also in it for the long haul, and five operational tours was a huge achievement for any dog. Ironically it was while I was driving to RAF Cosford for a Squadron meeting to decide on personnel for the next deployment to Afghanistan that I had to pull over to take a call from our Media Ops office. To be honest, I was getting a bit fed up of all the TV and newspaper interviews at this point, if only because I felt I had more important work to do for the RAF. By the time I got to Cosford, several phone calls had been made and I was told that I had to do one of the pending TV requests but I could choose which one. At the time I was fuming. The whole media thing was starting to take over my life and getting in the way of my job, but I've no idea why I was getting quite so upset about it.

The one who they really wanted to see, Buster, was totally cool about everything. Buster was unflappable. That was one if his incredible gifts when we were in Afghanistan and Iraq. His calmness in a crisis was so inspirational – one look at Buster and he put fear into perspective. If he didn't panic and run then there was no need for me to either. Buster was a great comfort to me in war and was still doing that for me in his retirement too. My dog had star quality and I needed to find my sparkle because I was not going to let Buster down.

Media Ops were back on the phone. They were still fielding calls from several TV channels requesting interviews, and I was being asked to please make up my mind. The next call came from Neil Furniss, one of my corporals at the Dog Section at RAF Waddington, who was very excited because he had just had a call from the BBC's *The One Show.* He said that Katherine Jenkins was going to be a guest as well, so I had bloody well get my arse over there. Turns out he had already accepted on my behalf! And to make sure we went, he insisted on driving Buster and me down to London. Media Ops were relieved a decision had been made.

We set off early one cold Thursday morning and headed to the studios. We were given the dressing room next to the *Top Gear* offices and, even though the main presenters were away filming in India, the crew got to hear that Buster was in the building and piled in to meet him. He was in his element once again and lapping up all the fuss. They called him war hero and special dog. I was so proud and we had only just arrived.

In rehearsal Buster was like a dog on speed. He sniffed and 'searched' around the studio, as normal, and I'm sure that put the crew at ease. But when all that was done we were just hanging around. Buster was bored and went into snooze mode – until we met Katherine Jenkins. She really is a beautiful woman and she was all-eyes for Buster. When we sat next to her on *The One Show* sofa she was fussing over Buster, and I'm sure Neil was really jealous as he watched from the wings. Katherine was happy to pose for a photo with us after the show too. It was all over far too quickly, and as we set off back to Waddo Tracy rang to tell us that Facebook was alive with messages from people wishing Buster all the best for the future and thanking him for keeping our soldiers safe in Afghanistan. She was really proud of both of us and hearing what other people thought of Buster (and me) brought it all home to her too.

Remembrance Day that year was especially busy for Buster and me. After appearing on *The One Show* and *BBC Breakfast,* we received an invitation from the RAF Police Association to take part in a parade at the National Memorial Arboretum in Staffordshire. It was another early morning for us but it was worth it just to see the faces of the people, especially the veterans, who had been waiting patiently to meet Buster. In his ceremonial coat and medals Buster was at the head of the parade leading the way to the Royal Military Police Memorial, where we all gathered in the cold and the rain to hear the names of our fallen comrades. It was an honour in which you could see Buster took great pride.

It was simply magic for me watching Buster take all the accolades in his stride. He was never fazed by the events or the attention of the people. He loved it. And when we got through to the final of the Crufts Friends for Life Award in 2012, we were left in no doubt at all that the life and times of Air Dog Buster really had captured the nation's hearts.

My friend Si Pound stepped forward to handle Buster for the event and do the promotional film, as I was due to be on a course in America, just before another detachment to Afghanistan. It was good of him to do that and he had served with Buster so knew how special he was. But I can't say I was disappointed when, at the last minute, my detachment was put back and I was able to go to Crufts with Buster after all.

I like the show because I love seeing people's reaction to the dogs and their work keeping our boys and girls safe in Afghanistan. Showcasing the work can help with recruitment to the RAF Police too. That year was important because we were also doing a capability demonstration in the main arena, which the audience loved. Buster and I waited in the wings while the team showed off the full power of the RAF dogs: from the guard and patrol to the bomb dogs. The team did the service proud and Buster just wanted to get out there and join them.

The lads and dogs lined up at the end of the display to a standing ovation and then, in the middle of it all, I marched on with Buster. It was then the announcement was made that Buster was retiring. When they read out his achievements and said he had saved countless lives during his five operational tours, the standing ovation got louder and louder. It was an incredible moment and I can tell you that there were a few rough, tough airmen in tears – over a dog.

Buster was on parade the entire four days of the show, but as the voting for the Friends for Life Award was building Buster was in great demand. Everyone was stopping us and asking for photos. I must have had the most photographed legs at Crufts that day. Buster was in his element posing in his red and black coat with stall holders and members of the public. But even Buster was ready for a rest after a few hours of the equivalent of a celebrity signing autographs. It had been a long and exhausting day meeting his adoring fans so I decided we would make our way back to the Hilton hotel where we were staying so he could have a rest in our room. He sat beautifully still while I took off his special coat and his medals and then he wandered over to his dog bed, circled it a few times and then flopped and sighed. I knew how he felt.

I went down to meet friends, Phil Brown and Pinky Penman, the other two provost marshals' dog inspectors, and Flight Lieutenant Mick Larkman MBE, the officer in charge of dogs in the RAF. I was just about to order some food when Phil got a phone call. The organisers of Friends for Life wanted a rehearsal. I made my way back to the arena. I then met the other finalists, Phil, a civilian policeman whose dog Obi had been injured in the Tottenham riots; Steve, an ex-Royal Navy man and his assistance dog Kizzie; Karen, who had been helped through depression by her dog

Ruby; and the mother of Laura, a blind Paralympic cyclist who was away training, and Laura's dog Libby. We ran through the order of things and we all received a trophy for reaching the finals. A lovely touch, I thought. It made us all feel like winners.

I made my way back to the hotel to pick up on the meal and pint and a conversation about the charity we would support if Buster happened to win the public vote. It was a unanimous decision: the recently formed charity Hounds for Heroes.

That important decision made, I went upstairs to collect Buster for his walk before bedtime. I opened the door and called his name – nothing. I turned the light on and walked in the room. I looked towards the window, fearing the worst, but I knew there were safety rails so he must be in the room somewhere.

And where was this special dog? Buster was actually under the duvet with his head on the pillow. I called his name and he briefly lifted his head, before settling back down. He didn't move all night. Luckily it was a twin room and I had my own bed. We were both too tired to put up with a reminder of the days sharing a mozzipod.

The next day was much of the same. At one point, though, I did feel very awkward. Buster and I were walking past one of the stalls where the staff and volunteers were rooting for Steve and his dog Kizzie, they even had leaflets printed with the number to vote. They were doing a great job for Steve and Kizzie but as soon as people saw Buster in his coat and medals they were down on the floor giving him lots of cuddles. One lady shouted out, 'Buster, I've voted for you!' and suddenly there was a Buster fan club gathered by Steve's stand. I couldn't help but mouth a 'sorry' to their hard-working volunteers.

On the evening of the final day, everyone was buzzing about the voting and there was big excitement in Buster's camp. When the nominees gathered in reception for a final briefing, Phil, the civilian policeman said, 'All my mates have voted for Buster. Five tours for a dog, you can't beat that.' I felt very humbled.

It was time to go into the arena and hear the result of the vote. All day the public had had the chance to vote for their favourite story and now was the moment of truth. Buster and I got into our allotted position at the rear of the main arena and waited to walk out.

'OK, Buster, it's us next so best behaviour please, because everyone will be looking at you.' I made a few adjustments to my uniform and donned my distinctive RAF Police cap.

Phil and Obi were the first out and received rapturous applause. It was Buster and me next and as we were called, we set off marching. As we marched smartly out into the arena, I noticed that the entire audience was on its feet. I hoped out loud that we had won. I saw Buster raise his head just that little bit higher, and as the applause built I'm sure he grew taller and taller, and I'm sure he knew all the clapping was for him, not me.

When all the finalists were in the arena it was time for the announcement. There was a hush around the stadium as everyone waited to hear who had won. Buster was beautifully still at my feet, despite the excitement of the occasion, and I couldn't help but feel so proud of him at that moment – whatever the result.

'The Friends for Life award 2012 goes to ... Will and Buster.'

I dropped down to Buster and gave him the biggest hug ever. The crowd were clapping and cheering like mad. Buster's tail was wagging like crazy and I'm sure he knew all eyes were on him.

Jennifer Saunders presented the trophy to me and Clare Balding came over for a chat. When she asked me what the award meant to me, I wanted to thank everyone as they had given Buster a fantastic end to a fantastic career.

We were presented with a cheque for £1,500 which was instantly given to the charity Hounds for Heroes, and we marched off to another standing ovation. What a perfect end for the little man. To show his appreciation, Buster started barking as if he wanted to thank everyone himself. He was so excited and gave the crowd his best bark with his ears in full flap.

As we left the arena, I checked my phone, which had been on silent the whole time. It was flashing Tracy's name. She had been watching the ceremony on her computer in Cyprus and was in tears. She wanted to talk to Buster and he was happy to bark a few messages down the mobile.

Out of the arena we were instantly mobbed by people wanting their photograph taken with Buster. Even I got in the odd shot. Once again the chaos started with everyone wanting us to appear on TV and do interviews. But we had one problem: Buster was booked to leave for Cyprus the following morning. We were going to our new home, where I would continue my work as a trainer of dogs and their handlers – and back to Tracy, at last.

ITV breakfast agreed to come over to Brize Norton before we left, so we had another early start. At 0600 the next morning I was in my best uniform and collecting Buster for his next moment of stardom. It was freezing outside and we were hanging around for ages, as is pretty much the norm for TV things, I've learned. Allen Parton, the founder of Hounds for Heroes, his dog EJ and Squadron Leader Wayne Palmer were meeting us on the airfield to accept our winner's cheque officially, before Buster headed off to start his retirement in the sun.

It was worth bearing the cold for the TV people and it was great to hear that Allen Parton was going to put our donation towards the training of the first six puppies destined to assist injured men and women from all three Armed Forces plus the Police and Fire Service. Buster got on well with Allen's own assistance dog EJ and it was good to see the two of them sniffing and snuffling around. It would be Buster's last chance to get his nose near English soil for quite some time and he was making the most of it.

Later that day, my colleague Phil Brown, who would also be on our flight out to Cyprus, gave Buster a final leg stretch while I checked our bags in to the terminal. At the time Monarch airlines were being used as charter flights to Cyprus to free the military aircraft for use in Afghanistan, and the captain of the plane appeared at the top of the steps and asked, 'Is that Buster, the dog off the telly?'

Phil said he was that very dog and the next minute Buster was invited onto the flight deck, where he was introduced to all the crew and had his photograph taken. Buster naturally obliged and gave everyone the full works, with the adoring eyes, the smiles, nuzzles and classic regal Buster stance.

While I was checking Buster's accommodation in the hold, Phil came down and found me.

'Come and look at this,' he said. I got my belongings and followed him to the front of the plane. There on the front row lay Buster, being fussed by two stewardesses! He'd been so well behaved that the captain had insisted he should travel in the cabin with the rest of us. It was a lovely idea but totally against regulations so Buster had to say his goodbyes. But he didn't miss out on his own in-flight meal of sausages in gravy!

When we landed in Cyprus, Tracy was there to meet us and she brought Daggo and Little Buster along too, who were going mad to see their slightly odd big brother. It was wonderful to be reunited as a family once more.

Afterword

And so officially began Buster's retirement. Never before has a dog deserved his retirement in the sun as much as Buster, and so close to his favourite place – the beach. Right from the start I knew he was special, and having this great chunk of a dog alongside me is something I have come to rely on.

Thousands of lives have been saved by this spaniel. He is a best friend in dog's clothing. An RAF dog with his mossy feet firmly on the ground. A brave dog who has served his colleagues and his country with unstinting devotion. A dog in a million.

I'm proud of Buster, and proud to know him and proud to hear him praised by colleagues. And this still happens: even though he's retired, he's remembered for all the lives he saved.

I know how lucky I was to have Buster by my side in conflict. I was never alone, as others were alone. He has always looked as if he understood all I said, and I've found great comfort in that, especially when there was no one else I could talk to, no one who could just listen. He bridged the gap when I was missing loved ones and it's a gap that widens – especially when you're being shot at.

We made a pact from the start to look after each other, and Buster has stayed true to our bargain. He saved my life every day we were together. I owe him so much that I can never repay the debt, even if we both lived forever.

I'm just glad he is now home, so we never have to be parted again.

My war dog, my hero, my friend – Buster.

Acknowledgements

There are so many people to thank for their support that the acknowledgements could run into another book. I have been extremely fortunate to meet so many extraordinary people: men and women who are prepared to give so much of themselves. I want to thank A Company 2nd Battalion the MERCIAN Regiment, especially Sergeant Michael 'Locky' Lockett MC and Captain Rupert Bowers MiD. May they rest in peace. Lance Corporal 'Chan' Chandler MiD and the men of the Viking Troop Royal Marines who kept us safe when surrounded by danger. My thanks also to the Coldstream Guards and all military working dogs and their handlers. Tracy and all my family and friends for their unwavering support. And last, but by no means least, the hairy fella himself, my pal Buster. Thank you Buster, you are a dog in a million and the protector of thousands. I salute you.